BIG GUYS DON'T SHRINK

BIG GUYS DO

Compiled by ERIC ZWEIG

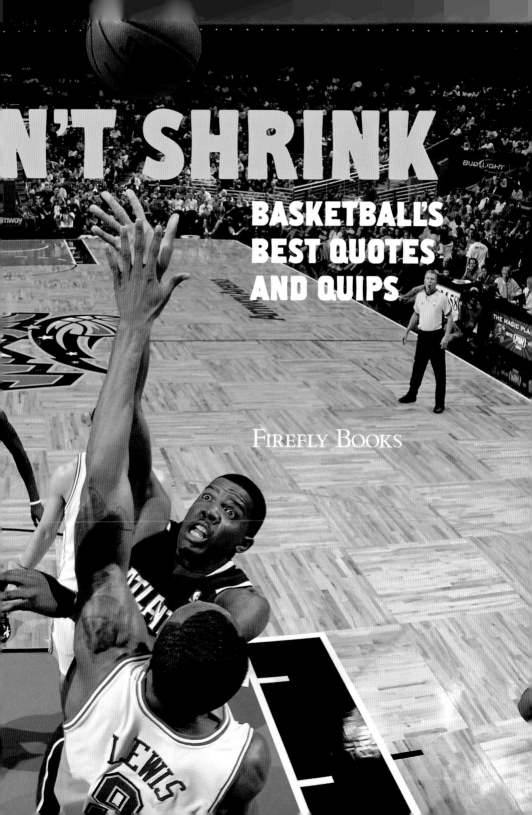

N'T SHRINK

BASKETBALL'S BEST QUOTES AND QUIPS

Firefly Books

A FIREFLY BOOK

Published by Firefly Books Ltd. 2008

First printing

PUBLISHER CATALOGING-IN-PUBLICATION DATA (U.S.)
Zweig, Eric, 1963-
Big guys don't shrink : basketball's best quotes and quips / Eric Zweig.
[176] p. : photos. (chiefly col.) ;   cm.
Includes index.
Summary: Compilation of quotes about basketball,
including quotes from the National Basketball Association.
ISBN-13: 978-1-55407-386-3 (pbk.)
ISBN-10: 1-55407-386-3
1. Basketball — Quotations, maxims, etc. 2. Basketball – Humor.
3. National Basketball Association – Quotations, maxims, etc. 4. Basketball – Humor. I. Title.
796.323 dc22   GV885.13Z95 2008

LIBRARY AND ARCHIVES CANADA CATALOGUING IN PUBLICATION
Zweig, Eric, 1963-
Big guys don't shrink : basketball's best quotes and quips / Eric Zweig.
Includes index.
ISBN-13: 978-1-55407-386-3 :c$17.95
ISBN-10: 1-55407-386-3
1. Basketball—Quotations, maxims, etc. 2. Basketball—Humor.
3. National Basketball Association—Quotations, maxims, etc.
4. National Basketball Association—Humor. I. Title.
GV885.13.Z84 2008   796.323   C2008-901789-7

Published in the United States by
Firefly Books (U.S.) Inc.
P.O. Box 1338, Ellicott Station
Buffalo, New York 14205

Published in Canada by
Firefly Books Ltd.
66 Leek Crescent
Richmond Hill, Ontario L4B 1H1

Cover and interior design by Sari Naworynski

Printed in China

The publisher gratefully acknowledges the financial support for our publishing program by the Government of Canada through the Book Publishing Industry Development Program.

*For Mike C., Rod, Mitch, Mike M., Greg, Angus,
David and Toni... And everyone else in the
Digital Media newsroom.*

CONTENTS

INTRODUCTION

"I'm not talking any more. That's it. No more words. It's over. Wanna know the deal? Mum is the word here. My game talks and conversation walks... I'm basically a quiet guy who keeps to himself. I don't like to talk."

NBA journeyman Edgar Jones, unable to maintain his vow of silence even while making it.

You just know there must have been media people listening to this who were dying to say – like Yosemite Sam or Rocky the Gangster to Bugs Bunny – "Shut up shutting up." Fortunately for me, no one ever says that to professional athletes. If they did, there's no way that I would now have compiled five different sports titles for this series of books!

I'll be honest. Basketball is not my favorite sport. Not to play, anyway. I've enjoyed watching it over the years (especially during the time of Magic Johnson and Larry Bird), but I am a horrible basketball player. Ever since I saw an open lane to the basket, grabbed the ball and made a football-style run for it in a grade school game, I have known that basketball was not the sport for me. Which was something of a shame, given that I grew fairly tall at a pretty young age.

Of course, 6 foot 1 is only pretty tall in the real world. I was certainly taller than any of my friends, but I knew I was only as tall as the Boston Celtics' Nate Archibald, and they called him Tiny! That kind of kept things in perspective. On the other hand, I am actually taller than the only NBA player I have ever met in person. Vinnie Johnson of the Detroit Pistons was called The Microwave because "he heats up fast" when he came in off the bench. Websites list him as 6 foot 2, but I swear he was shorter than I am.

Despite my lack of basketball prowess, I have twice been mistaken for Kevin McHale. Admittedly, neither occurrence came on the court. The first time probably doesn't count as I think it was actually a joking reference to the way we both bounce when we walk. But the second time a hotel clerk in suburban Detroit did a double take before telling me he'd thought I was Kevin McHale. Now that's just crazy talk really! McHale is 6 foot 10 and about the only thing we actually have in common is white skin and dark hair.

Being only a casual basketball fan I wasn't really sure if I would find the same treasure trove of offbeat remarks I had found for my books about other sports. I needn't have worried. Even if there had been nothing else, the frustrated offerings of a parade of burned-out basketball coaches from the college and professional ranks could probably have filled a book. "I always mean what I say," University of North Carolina coaching legend Dean Smith once confided, "but I don't always say what I'm thinking." Fortunately, there are lots of others who seem only too happy to spout off every thought that comes into their heads!

Among players, Shaquille O'Neal and Charles Barkley (now an outspoken broadcaster) are particularly vocal, and usually hilarious. In a sport like basketball, though, mere words aren't always enough. "I feel bad," said Cleveland Cavaliers coach Mike Brown, "that my words don't do justice to what he did," after LeBron James scored 29 of his team's last 30 points in a double-overtime playoff victory in 2007.

This book isn't quite as exciting as that, but I hope you'll enjoy it.

"There are really only two plays: *Romeo and Juliet* and put the darn ball in the basket."

LONGTIME NCAA COACH **ABE LEMONS**

"The only difference between a good shot and a bad shot is if it goes in or not."

NBA STAR TURNED BROADCASTER **CHARLES BARKLEY**

"Winning is like deodorant – it comes up and a lot of things don't stink."

NEW YORK KNICKS GUARD (AND CURRENT BOSTON CELTICS COACH) **GLENN "DOC" RIVERS**

"When I was losing, they called me nuts. When I was winning, they called me eccentric."

TV ANALYST AND FORMER MARQUETTE UNIVERSITY COACH **AL McGUIRE**

"Finish last in your league and they call you idiot. Finish last in medical school and they call you doctor."

FAMED NCAA COACH **ABE LEMONS**

"I keep both eyes on my man. The basket hasn't moved on me yet."

BASKETBALL SUPERSTAR **JULIUS ERVING**

"Sometimes that light at the end of the tunnel is a train."

NBA LEGEND AND BROADCASTER **CHARLES BARKLEY**

They say that nobody is perfect. Then they tell you practice makes perfect. I wish they'd make up their minds.

NBA LEGEND WILT CHAMBERLAIN

"The opera isn't over till the fat lady sings."

WASHINGTON BULLETS COACH **DICK MOTTA** EXPLAINING
WHY HIS TEAM STILL HAD A CHANCE, EVEN AFTER FALLING
BEHIND IN A PLAYOFF SERIES

"If a guy pays you five dollars, you give him seven dollars worth of work."

BOSTON CELTICS LEGEND BILL RUSSELL

"Great effort springs naturally from a great attitude."

MIAMI HEAT COACH **PAT RILEY**

"I hate All-Star games – the whole goofing around and not playing hard thing. I enjoy it much more when you take it seriously."

PHOENIX SUNS STAR **STEVE NASH**

"A winner is someone who recognizes his God-given talents, works his tail off to develop them into skills and uses these skills to accomplish his goals."

BOSTON CELTICS SUPERSTAR **LARRY BIRD**

"Good teams become great ones when the members trust each other enough to surrender the 'me' for the 'we.'"

LONGTIME CHICAGO BULLS AND LOS ANGELES LAKERS COACH **PHIL JACKSON**

"You shouldn't just work on your jump shot. You should work on being a better person, a better teammate and a better friend."

STAR WOMEN'S PLAYER AND COACH **SUE WICKS**

"Ability may get you to the top, but it takes character to keep you there."

LEGENDARY UCLA COACH **JOHN WOODEN**

"I can't judge them on how we played. We couldn't have beaten the Pismo Beach Panthers tonight."

GOLDEN STATE WARRIORS COACH **DON NELSON**, WHEN ASKED TO APPRAISE THE 2007-08 BOSTON CELTICS AFTER THEY HAD JUST BEATEN HIS TEAM 105-82

"They called us the Cinderella team, and we played like we were going to turn into a pumpkin."

OHIO STATE COACH **FRED TAYLOR** EXPLAINS AN 80-66 LOSS TO NORTH CAROLINA IN THE NCAA TOURNAMENT

"At Pan American one year the only player coming back was named Tree McCullough. But hell, his name could have been Stumpy."

LONGTIME NCAA COACH **ABE LEMONS**

"They dribble faster than we run without the ball."

UNIVERSITY OF TEXAS COACH **BOB WELTLICH** AFTER AN 84-67 LOSS TO ARKANSAS

"This year we plan to run and shoot. Next season we hope to run and score."

UNIVERSITY OF OKLAHOMA COACH **BILLY TUBBS**

"He has the shooting range. What he doesn't have is the making range."

PRINCETON COACH **PETE CARRIL** ON WHY HE WOULDN'T MOVE STEVE GOODRICH FROM CENTER TO FORWARD

"We are not the LSU Tigers – we're the LSU
Somnambulists."

LOUISIANA STATE UNIVERSITY COACH **DALE BROWN** AFTER
A LETHARGIC VICTORY OVER THE UNIVERSITY OF ALABAMA

"I'm trying to do too much and I'm thinking too much
and I'm thinking about trying to do too much."

UNIVERSITY OF KANSAS GUARD **TONY GUY** TRIES TO
EXPLAIN HIS SHOOTING SLUMP

**"If you can figure it out,
I'm going to tell you to resign,
and I will double your salary
to sit on the bench."**

TORONTO RAPTORS COACH **SAM MITCHELL**, WHEN ASKED
WHAT IT WOULD TAKE TO MAKE THE INCONSISTENT JOEY
GRAHAM CONSISTENTLY GOOD

"We're going to wear black patches on our jerseys
next season because our defense died."

CENTENARY COLLEGE COACH **TOMMY CANTERBURY**

"We can alley, but we don't have the oop."

OKLAHOMA CITY UNIVERSITY COACH **ABE LEMONS**
EXPLAINS WHY HIS TEAM MESSED UP AN ALLEY-OOP
ATTEMPT

"Don't put me back in."

UNIVERSITY OF MEMPHIS GUARD ANTONIO ANDERSON TO
COACH JOHN CALIPARI WHILE WATCHING BACKUP DONEAL
MACK MAKE SEVEN THREE-POINTERS IN THE SECOND HALF

"That's part of the challenge of being a professional athlete."

HOUSTON ROCKETS BACKUP CENTER JOHN AMAECHI ON
NOT HAVING PLAYED A SINGLE MINUTE ALL SEASON

"Coming off the bench is tough. As soon as you don't produce, the starters are coming back."

TORONTO RAPTOR KRIS HUMPHRIES

"I don't want some turkey to look good and then have to play him the next five games."

UNIVERSITY OF TEXAS COACH ABE LEMONS EXPLAINING
WHY HE DIDN'T LIKE TO MAKE PLAYER SUBSTITUTIONS
WHEN HIS TEAM WAS LOSING

"I was afraid the team would win without me."

FORMER MARQUETTE UNIVERSITY COACH AND BROADCASTER
AL McGUIRE ADMITTED HE USED TO GET ON THE REFEREES
BUT EXPLAINS WHY HE TRIED NOT TO GET EJECTED

"He doesn't shine them. He sends them through a car wash."

UCLA STAR **LYNN SHACKELFORD** ON BOB LANIER'S
SIZE 22 SHOES

"I am 7 feet 4 with my shoes on, and I always play with my shoes on."

WHY U.S. OLYMPIC BASKETBALL TEAM CENTER
TOM BURLESON WASN'T BOTHERED BY REPORTS THAT
HE WAS ONLY 7 FEET 2 WHEN MEASURED BAREFOOT

"He changes your shots when he's in the game. He also changes your shots when he's out of the game because you get so used to trying to throw it over him, you forget when he's not there."

11-YEAR NBA VETERAN **CLIFF LEVINGSTON** ON PLAYING
AGAINST 7-FOOT-4 UTAH JAZZ CENTER MARK EATON

"I don't know how Gasol blocked this shot, but he did. He's long."

DALLAS MAVERICKS GUARD **JASON TERRY** ON THE MEMPHIS
GRIZZLIES 7-FOOT POWER FORWARD PAU GASOL

"Being 7 feet 2 helps."

CLEVELAND CAVALIERS CENTER **ZYDRUNAS ILGAUSKAS**
AFTER MOVING INTO THE TOP 100 ALL-TIME IN REBOUNDING

"He's big. That's how he gets all those shots."

OHIO STATE 7-FOOTER **GREG ODEN** ON GEORGETOWN'S
7-FOOT-2 ROY HIBBERT

"Charles joined my family for a day at the beach last summer, and my children asked if they could go in the ocean. I had to tell them, 'Not right now, kids. Charles is using it.'"

PHILADELPHIA 76ERS GENERAL MANAGER **PAT WILLIAMS**
ON 260-POUND ROOKIE CHARLES BARKLEY

"No, ma'am. I'm a jockey for a dinosaur."

6-FOOT-9 CHICAGO BULLS CENTER **JOHNNY KERR**,
WHEN ASKED IF HE WAS A BASKETBALL PLAYER

"No, I clean giraffe ears."

6-FOOT-10 WASHINGTON BULLETS **STAR ELVIN HAYES**,
WHEN ASKED IF HE WAS A BASKETBALL PLAYER

"Here's a 6-foot-10 guy in sneakers and the lady's asking me, 'Profession?'"

CINCINNATI ROYALS COACH **JACK McMAHON** AFTER
RUSHING NATE BOWMAN TO THE HOSPITAL WITH A
DISLOCATED ANKLE

"I got bald."

PHILADELPHIA 76ERS COACH **ALEX HANNUM**, WHEN ASKED
WHY HE WAS LISTED AT 6 FOOT 8 AS A PLAYER BUT ONLY
6 FOOT 7 AS A COACH

"They measured me when I was sitting down."

SUDANESE-BORN 7-FOOT-7 NBA STAR MANUTE BOL ON WHY
HIS PASSPORT LISTED HIM AT 5 FOOT 2

"My mother had to send me to the movies with my birth certificate so that I wouldn't have to pay the extra 50 cents that the adults had to pay."

NBA SUPERSTAR **KAREEM ABDUL-JABBAR**

"When everybody else is tired, he's still going to be tall."

SEATTLE SUPERSONICS FORWARD **LEONARD GRAY** ON 7-FOOT-4 TEAMMATE TOM BURLESON

"Quick guys get tired. Big guys don't shrink."

WHY UNIVERSITY OF WASHINGTON COACH **MARV HARSHMAN** PREFERRED SIZE TO SPEED

"Any American boy can be a basketball star if he grows up, up, up."

COLUMNIST AND AUTHOR **BILL VAUGHN**

"You can run a lot of plays when your X is twice as big as the other guy's O. It makes your Xs and Os pretty good."

NBA PLAYER TURNED COACH **PAUL WESTPHAL**

"Everybody pulls for David, nobody roots for Goliath."

NBA LEGEND **WILT CHAMBERLAIN**

"**Red used to never have a curfew.** I asked him why he never had a curfew. He said, 'Because I have to be there to **enforce it.**'"

NBA HALL OF FAMER BILL RUSSELL ON WHAT IT WAS LIKE
ON THE ROAD WITH THE CELTICS UNDER LEGENDARY COACH
RED AUERBACH

"If I make a set of rules, then a guy goes out and steals an airplane. He comes back and says, 'It wasn't on the list of rules.'"

OKLAHOMA CITY UNIVERSITY COACH ABE LEMONS EXPLAINS
WHY HE DIDN'T LIKE TO HAVE A LOT OF TEAM RULES

"My training rule is 'don't get caught.'"

UNIVERSITY OF SOUTH CAROLINA COACH FRANK McGUIRE

"I want my teams to have my personality – surly, obnoxious and arrogant."

MARQUETTE COACH AL McGUIRE

" I'll always remember Tom Heinsohn's pep talks. One time there were 72 bleeps in it – and that was Christmas Day. "

FORMER BOSTON CELTICS GUARD PAUL WESTPHAL
REMEMBERS HIS COACH

"We were a team with a lot of lacks, but Sharman fit us together perfectly."

LOS ANGELES LAKERS STAR JERRY WEST ON COACH BILL
SHARMAN FOLLOWING THE LAKERS' 1972 NBA TITLE

"We have black players, white players, a Mormon and four Yugoslavians. Our toughest decision isn't what offense or defense to run but what type of warm-up music to play."

WAGNER COLLEGE COACH TIM CAPSTRAW

"When a coach is hired, he's fired. The date just hasn't been filled in yet."

UNIVERSITY OF ALABAMA COACH C.M. NEWTON

"I'm like Rudolph the Red-Nosed Reindeer. If I'm not ready, the sled isn't going to go."

MINNESOTA TIMBERWOLVES STAR **KEVIN GARNETT**

"All right, who's playing for second?"

BOSTON CELTICS LEGEND **LARRY BIRD** BEFORE A THREE-POINT SHOOTING CONTEST

"I'll always be number one to myself."

NBA GREAT **MOSES MALONE**

"I'd pay to see me play."

WASHINGTON BULLETS FUTURE HALL OF FAMER **ELVIN HAYES**

"One of my other nicknames was Thomas Edison because I invented so many moves. "

NBA LEGEND **EARL "THE PEARL" MONROE**

"I said I was going to light it up like Las Vegas in Cleveland."

CLEVELAND CAVALIERS STAR **LEBRON JAMES** RECALLING WHAT HE HAD SAID WHEN THE CAVS PICKED HIM FIRST IN THE 2003 DRAFT, AFTER LEADING THE TEAM INTO THE 2007 NBA FINAL

"These young guys are playing checkers. I'm out there playing chess."

LOS ANGELES LAKERS STAR KOBE BRYANT

"A man has to know his limitations, and I don't have any."

NBA JOURNEYMAN EDGAR JONES

"Everything is going right for me, and I just feel like I'm out there by myself. Like in practice when you're by yourself and working out."

CLEVELAND CAVALIERS STAR LEBRON JAMES AFTER SCORING 24 POINTS IN THE FOURTH QUARTER TO RALLY HIS TEAM FROM A 20-POINT DEFICIT TO BEAT THE TORONTO RAPTORS

"What excites me the most is when a coach calls a time-out and chews out his forward because I just dunked on his head."

UTAH JAZZ SUPERSTAR KARL MALONE

"When you go out there and do the things you're supposed to do, people view you as selfish."

NBA LEGEND WILT CHAMBERLAIN

"There is no 'I' in team but there is in win."

CHICAGO BULLS SUPERSTAR MICHAEL JORDAN

"The extra pass and the extra effort on defense always get the job done."

NBA LEGEND KAREEM ABDUL-JABBAR

"The idea is not to block every shot. The idea is to make your opponent believe that you might block every shot."

BOSTON CELTICS LEGEND BILL RUSSELL

"My coach predicated everything on defense. He always talked about defense, defense, defense. I took it to heart that if you play defense, you can take the heart from an offensive player."

NBA JOURNEYMAN ERIC WILLIAMS

"We would set up a zone defense that had four men around the key, and I guarded the basket. When the other team took a shot, I'd just go up and tap it out."

BASKETBALL LEGEND GEORGE MIKAN, THE GAME'S FIRST "BIG MAN" AT 6 FOOT 10, AND THE REASON GOALTENDING WAS MADE ILLEGAL

"Basketball is like war, in that offensive weapons are developed first, and it always takes a while for the defense to catch up."

LEGENDARY BOSTON CELTICS COACH RED AUERBACH

"It's like all guys want to do is make a dunk, grab their shirt and yell out and scream —

they could be down 30 points but that's what they do. Okay, so you made a dunk. Get back down the floor on defense!"

NBA LEGEND OSCAR ROBERTSON

"It's the little details that are vital. Little things make big things happen."

NCAA COACHING LEGEND **JOHN WOODEN**

"I try to do the right thing at the right time. They may just be little things, but usually they make the difference between winning and losing."

KAREEM ABDUL-JABBAR

"Just be patient. Let the game come to you. Don't rush. Be quick, but don't hurry."

NBA HALL OF FAMER **EARL "THE PEARL" MONROE**

"If you don't have time to do it right, when will you have time to do it over?"

LONGTIME UCLA COACH **JOHN WOODEN**

"We have 11 defenses to stop him, but he has **45** ways to score."

GOLDEN STATE WARRIORS COACH AL ATTLES ON NATE "TINY" ARCHIBALD

"My biggest thrill came the night Elgin Baylor and I combined for 73 points in Madison Square Garden. Elgin had 71 of them."

FORMER LOS ANGELES LAKER **"HOT" ROD HUNDLEY**

"We're going to turn this team around 360 degrees."

NEW YORK NETS STAR **JASON KIDD**

"Going into the series I thought Michael had 2,000 moves. I was wrong. He has 3,000."

PHOENIX TRAIL BLAZERS STAR **CLYDE DREXLER** ON MICHAEL JORDAN, AFTER JORDAN'S CHICAGO BULLS BEAT THE BLAZERS FOR THE 1992 NBA CHAMPIONSHIP

"We're shooting 100 percent – 60 percent from the field and 40 percent from the free-throw line."

UNIVERSITY OF MISSOURI COACH **NORM STEWART**

"Chemistry is a class you take in high school or college where you figure out two plus two is 10 or something."

NBA STAR **DENNIS RODMAN**

"We all get heavier as we get older because there's a lot more information in our heads. Our heads weigh more."

LOS ANGELES LAKERS CENTER
VLADE DIVAC EXPLAINS WHY
HE REPORTED TO TRAINING
CAMP 15 POUNDS HEAVIER

"There's no such thing as coulda, shoulda and woulda. If you shoulda and coulda, you woulda done it."

LOS ANGELES LAKERS COACH **PAT RILEY**

"The last time I checked, they had to get up the same time we did."

TORONTO RAPTORS COACH **SAM MITCHELL** REFUSES TO USE THE EARLY START TIME AS AN EXCUSE FOR A LOSS TO THE NEW YORK KNICKS

"A lot of bad things happened to us. First, Auburn played well."

LONGTIME VANDERBILT COACH **C.M. NEWTON** EXPLAINS A LOSS TO AUBURN

"I was hoping Vanderbilt wouldn't bring their 'A' game and that we'd have a shot."

UNIVERSITY OF MASSACHUSETTS COACH **TRAVIS FORD** AFTER VANDERBILT SCORED 61 POINTS IN THE SECOND HALF FOR A 97–88 VICTORY

"Our wings began to ice."

KANSAS STATE COACH **JACK HARTMAN** EXPLAINS HOW HIS TEAM BLEW A 14-POINT LEAD AND LOST TO IOWA STATE

"We were a little sluggish. No, we were a lot sluggish."

SAN DIEGO CLIPPERS FORWARD **TERRY CUMMINGS** EXPLAINS A 17-POINT LOSS TO THE DALLAS MAVERICKS

"We were the quintessence of athletic atrocity."

HOUSTON ROCKETS GUARD MIKE NEWLIN

"We lost it above the shoulders."

COACH BILL RUSSELL AFTER HIS SEATTLE SUPERSONICS
ABANDONED THE GAME PLAN DURING A LOSS TO THE
BOSTON CELTICS

"I think this whole game hinged on one call – the
one I made last April scheduling this game."

UNIVERSITY OF MAINE COACH PETER GAVETT ON A
SEASON-OPENING 115-57 LOSS TO 7-FOOT-4 CENTER RALPH
SAMPSON AND THE UNIVERSITY OF VIRGINIA CAVALIERS

"The worst thing our players did was fail to
grow taller."

DUKE UNIVERSITY WOMEN'S BASKETBALL COACH
DEBBIE LEONARD AFTER A 103-39 LOSS

"I designed the play without realizing what big feet Larry has. I should have moved him over 6 inches in my diagram."

KANSAS CITY KINGS COACH PHIL JOHNSON AFTER GUARD LARRY DREW STEPPED ON THE OUT-OF-BOUNDS LINE, NULLIFYING A LAST-SECOND SHOT THAT WOULD HAVE BEATEN THE HOUSTON ROCKETS

"I bought a Stairmaster. I stare at it every day."

NBA STAR AND TV COMMENTATOR **CHARLES BARKLEY**
ON EXERCISE

"It's hard to be fit as a fiddle when you're shaped like a cello."

UTAH JAZZ COACH **FRANK LAYDEN** EXPLAINS WHY HE
WAS TRYING TO GET A 300-POUND PLAYER TO SLIM DOWN

"There are a lot of guys who can bench-press 300 pounds who couldn't play dead in a cowboy movie."

UNIVERSITY OF TEXAS COACH **RICK BARNES** ON THE
ALLEGED LACK OF STRENGTH OF 2007 NCAA PLAYER OF
THE YEAR, KEVIN DURANT

"If I die, I want to be sick."

UNIVERSITY OF TEXAS COACH **ABE LEMONS** ON WHY HE
DIDN'T LIKE TO JOG

"You can't play if you're dead."

PHILADELPHIA 76ERS STAR **CHARLES BARKLEY** ON WHY HE
FINISHED LAST IN THE TEAM'S 2-MILE TRAINING CAMP RUN

"Failure is good. It's fertilizer. Everything I've learned about coaching, I've learned from making mistakes."

LONGTIME NCAA AND NBA COACH RICK PITINO

"What to do with a mistake – recognize it, admit it, learn from it, forget it."

UNIVERSITY OF NORTH CAROLINA COACHING LEGEND DEAN SMITH

" I can accept failure, but I can't accept not trying. "

CHICAGO BULLS LEGEND MICHAEL JORDAN

"We have to learn from this loss. It doesn't make us a terrible team."

WASHINGTON STATE GUARD DERRICK LOW AFTER HIS FOURTH-RANKED AND PREVIOUSLY UNBEATEN TEAM LOST TO UCLA, WASHINGTON'S 50TH LOSS IN 51 GAMES AT PAULEY PAVILLION

"If you're not making mistakes then you're not doing anything. I'm positive that a doer makes mistakes."

LEGENDARY UCLA COACH JOHN WOODEN

"Hearing the crowd was great. It made what little hair I have stand on end."

DENVER NUGGETS STAR **ALEX ENGLISH** RECALLS THE STANDING OVATION HE RECEIVED AFTER SCORING 54 POINTS AGAINST THE HOUSTON ROCKETS

"It's pretty strange seeing all the Miami fans wearing white attire during home play-off games. The idea is to create a 'white hot' crowd. To me, it looks like a convention of bakers."

SPORTSWRITER **ROSS ATKIN**

"With every 10 fans that miss me, there are probably 10 or more that wish they could shoot me."

UTAH JAZZ FORWARD **CARLOS BOOZER** IN 2007, ON HIS FIRST TRIP BACK TO CLEVELAND AFTER BOLTING THE TEAM THREE YEARS EARLIER FOR MORE MONEY

"Philadelphia is one of those cities that doesn't have patience for anybody... Philly stands for winning. Nothing else."

FORMER 76ER **DIKEMBE MUTOMBO** ON PHILADELPHIA'S NOTORIOUSLY TOUGH FANS

"In a strange sort of way, it always feels better to close it out on the road. That silence, like church."

DETROIT PISTONS GUARD **CHAUNCEY BILLUPS** AFTER THE PISTONS ELIMINATED THE BULLS IN CHICAGO DURING THE 2007 PLAYOFFS

"**I don't know what it feels like to wear a thong**, but I imagine it feels something like what we had on in the first half. **I feel violated.**"

LOS ANGELES LAKERS SUPERSTAR KOBE BRYANT AFTER THE LAKERS WORE THROWBACK JERSEYS AND SHORT-SHORTS IN A GAME AGAINST THE BOSTON CELTICS (WHO WORE THEIR REGULAR SHORTS AND ONLY THE THROWBACK JERSEYS) DURING THE 2007-08 SEASON

"You have a routine. That doesn't mean you're superstitious. I'm not superstitious like wearing the same drawers or anything like that."

CLEVELAND CAVALIERS SUPERSTAR LEBRON JAMES DESCRIBES HIS PREGAME RITUALS

"I wonder if Steve Nash, the NBA's Most Valuable Player, ever gets tired of brushing back his hair? It sure seems like a sweatband would help."

SPORTSWRITER ROSS ATKIN

"I liked the choreography, but I didn't care for the costumes."

TOMMY TUNE, 6-FOOT-6 1/2 BROADWAY SINGER-DANCER-ACTOR-DIRECTOR, EXPLAINS WHY HE NEVER CONSIDERED PLAYING BASKETBALL

"Typical NBA punch. In hockey, your own team would beat you up for that."

PHOENIX SUNS STAR (AND CANADIAN) **STEVE NASH** ON DENVER'S CARMELO ANTHONY THROWING A SUCKER PUNCH AND THEN BACKING AWAY DURING A FIGHT BETWEEN THE NUGGETS AND THE KNICKS

"I've developed a healthy respect for my teeth."

WHY UNIVERSITY OF ARKANSAS CENTER **JACK SCHULTE** AVOIDED A FIGHT

"I thought he was going to hit me first, so I hit him first."

WHY SEATTLE SUPERSONICS FORWARD **XAVIER McDANIEL** GOT INTO A FIGHT WITH KEVIN WILLIS OF THE ATLANTA HAWKS

"I threw a left hook, but I was backpedaling so fast it never got there."

FORMER BALTIMORE BULLET CENTER **BOB FERRY** GIVES HIS VERSION OF A FIGHT WITH WILT CHAMBERLAIN OF THE PHILADELPHIA 76ERS

"In this league, everybody's got a pretty face and they're trying to keep it that way."

LOS ANGELES LAKERS COACH **PHIL JACKSON** AFTER KOBE BRYANT WAS SUSPENDED FOR PUNCHING MINNESOTA'S MARKO JARIC

"I knew I was dog meat. Luckily, I'm the high-priced dog meat that everybody wants. I'm the good-quality dog meat. I'm the Alpo of the NBA."

NBA SUPERSTAR **SHAQUILLE O'NEAL**

"He's about as safe as me in a room full of cookies. If I'm in a room full of cookies, the cookies ain't got no damn chance."

NBA STAR AND BROADCASTER **CHARLES BARKLEY** ON NEW YORK KNICKS COACH ISIAH THOMAS'S JOB SECURITY AFTER A 45-POINT LOSS TO THE BOSTON CELTICS

"Look, guys say a lot of things, and I don't put too much credence in it. Maybe they got him on a day when his milk was too warm for his Coco Puffs."

MINNESOTA TIMBERWOLVES GENERAL MANAGER **KEVIN McHALE** ON A KEVIN GARNETT TIRADE IN AN ESPN MAGAZINE INTERVIEW

"They shot the ball well early. What comes out of the microwave hot doesn't always stay hot. I know because I eat bagels in the morning."

MIAMI HEAT STAR **SHAQUILLE O'NEAL**

"Don't get caught looking at the apple in case someone takes the ladder away."

TORONTO RAPTORS COACH **LENNY WILKINS** ON THE POSSIBILITY OF WINNING A DIVISION TITLE

"Saltwater taffy."

PORTLAND TRAIL BLAZERS CENTER **CALDWELL JONES**, WHEN ASKED TO NAME HIS FAVORITE SEAFOOD

"You put the toast in the toaster, and it ain't done until the toaster says, 'Ding.'"

NBA SUPERSTAR SHAQUILLE O'NEAL PONDERS WHEN
HE'D BE READY TO RETURN FROM AN INJURY

"My cholesterol level went down 30 percent while I recruited him."

TRENTON STATE COACH **KEVIN BANNON** RECALLS RECRUIT-
ING FUTURE NCAA DIVISION III CAREER SCORING LEADER
GREG GRANT, WHO HAD A SUMMER JOB AT A SEAFOOD
RESTAURANT

"They're really aggressive. They're like roaches on bread – you drop some on the floor and, boom, they're on it."

MINNESOTA TIMBERWOLVES FORWARD **KEVIN GARNETT**
ON THE MIAMI HEAT DEFENSE

"I'm just a caraway seed in the bakery of life."

XAVIER COACH **PETE GILLEN**

"The last time out was to take the sandwich orders."

UNIVERSITY OF MISSISSIPPI COACH **ED MURPHY** EXPLAINS
HIS TIME OUT WITH TWO MINUTES LEFT IN A GAME HIS TEAM
WAS TRAILING BY 20 POINTS

"We're supposed to stop eating when he stops? But what if we're still hungry? He may have had a snack before he came over."

1992 U.S. OLYMPIC "DREAM TEAM" MEMBER **CHARLES
BARKLEY** HAS CONCERNS ABOUT THE PROPER ETIQUETTE
AT DINNER WITH PRINCE RAINIER AT THE ROYAL PALACE IN
MONTE CARLO

Too much coffee. Too much coffee and Gatorade. It's a hell of a mix. If you're ever tired in the morning, just try that mix and tell me what you think.

MINNESOTA TIMBERWOLVES STAR KEVIN GARNETT

"When you're playing him, it's like going through the Tunnel of Love. All you feel is hands, knees and elbows all over you."

NEW YORK KNICKS STAR **WALT FRAZIER** ON WHY CHICAGO'S
JERRY SLOAN WAS SO TOUGH DEFENSIVELY

"Rice defends against the free throw as well as anybody I've ever seen."

TEXAS A&M BASKETBALL COACH **SHELBY METCALFE** AFTER
WATCHING BAYLOR UNIVERSITY MISS 19 OF 35 FREE THROWS
AGAINST RICE

" I've never coached a player who takes as much physical abuse as he does. He's a bull in a china shop, and all those pieces of china like to hit back. "

UNIVERSITY OF NORTH CAROLINA COACH **ROY WILLIAMS**
ON TAR HEELS FORWARD TYLER HANSBROUGH

"We defend against the free throw very well."

SAN FRANCISCO STATE COACH **LYLE DAMON** AFTER AN
OPPONENT SHOT ONLY 58 PERCENT FROM THE FOUL LINE

"Half of them were bad calls."

NBA LEGEND **KAREEM ABDUL-JABBAR** AFTER ESTABLISH-
ING A CAREER RECORD WITH 4,194 FOULS

"**It is unbelievably frustrating to remain in a rugged occupation with waning skills.**"

BOSTON CELTICS STAR DAVE COWENS ON HIS DECISION TO RETIRE

"I knew it was time to retire when I was driving down the lane and got called for a three-second violation."

FORMER NBA PLAYER AND COACH JOHNNY KERR

"I'm 36. I could have waved the towel too aggressively for all I know."

DALLAS MAVERICK SCOTT WILLIAMS, WHO WASN'T SURE HOW HE'D SUFFERED A SLIGHT STOMACH STRAIN

"I remember they were calling us old when I came in, and that was six years ago. We were fighting that then."

BOSTON CELTICS STAR JOHN HAVLICEK DURING THE TEAM'S 1960s DYNASTY

"I plan to be back, and I hope to be doing the same thing I'm doing right now."

LOS ANGELES LAKERS LEGEND KAREEM ABDUL-JABBAR DENYING RUMORS OF HIS RETIREMENT, WHILE SIPPING CHAMPAGNE AFTER BEATING THE BOSTON CELTICS FOR THE 1987 NBA TITLE IN HIS 18TH SEASON

"Even when I'm old and gray, I won't be able to play it, but I'll still love the game."

CHICAGO BULLS SUPERSTAR MICHAEL JORDAN

"**Everybody looks at how many years you play. They forget about what you do to slow down Father Time. You can't beat him, but you can sure slow him down.**"

36-YEAR-OLD UTAH JAZZ STAR KARL MALONE, WHO PLAYED UNTIL HE WAS 40

"**Yao Ming is basically what they call him, the Great Wall of China.** Once he gets the ball, he's pretty much **unstoppable.**"

CHARLOTTE BOBCATS FORWARD GERALD WALLACE ON THE
HOUSTON ROCKETS' CHINESE SUPERSTAR

"Think of a 7-foot-5 Dirk Nowitzki who could pass the ball like Larry Bird."

DALLAS MAVERICKS PRESIDENT DONNIE NELSON DESCRIBES LITHUANIAN GIANT ARVYDAS SABONIS WHEN HE WAS IN HIS PRIME WITH THE SOVIET NATIONAL TEAM

"We're experts at bouncin', not pronouncin'."

GEESE AUSBIE OF THE HARLEM GLOBETROTTERS HAS DIFFICULTIES WITH THE NAME OF CHINESE DEPUTY PREMIER TENG HSIAO-PING

"Then you'd know what I was saying to you."

UNIVERSITY OF INDIANA CENTER UWE BLAB EXPLAINING TO COACH BOBBY KNIGHT WHY HE WOULDN'T GIVE HIM ANY GERMAN SWEAR WORDS TO USE ON THE REFEREES

"When our buildings get 10 years old they start falling apart. They've got buildings here been standing for 1,500 years. In Minnesota we had two seasons, winter and road construction. They've got cobblestone streets over here that last 700 years."

TORONTO RAPTORS COACH SAM MITCHELL MARVELS AT ITALY'S CULTURE AND HISTORY ON HIS TEAM'S VISIT TO ROME FOR ITS 2007-08 TRAINING CAMP

"It's an unbelievable situation when 25,000 people are booing you and throwing garbage at you. It's like the whole country was Notre Dame."

MARQUETTE BASKETBALL PLAYER JEROME WHITEHEAD AFTER A TOUR OF BRAZIL

"Prepare for every game like you just lost your last game."

LONGTIME NBA AND NCAA COACH LON KRUGER

" Be a dreamer. If you don't know how to dream, you're dead."

NORTH CAROLINA STATE COACH JIM VALVANO

"When you lose a 'must' game, it wasn't a 'must' game."

NEW YORK KNICKS TRAINER DANNY WHELAN

"You can't let praise or criticism get to you. It's a weakness to get caught up in either one."

UCLA COACH JOHN WOODEN

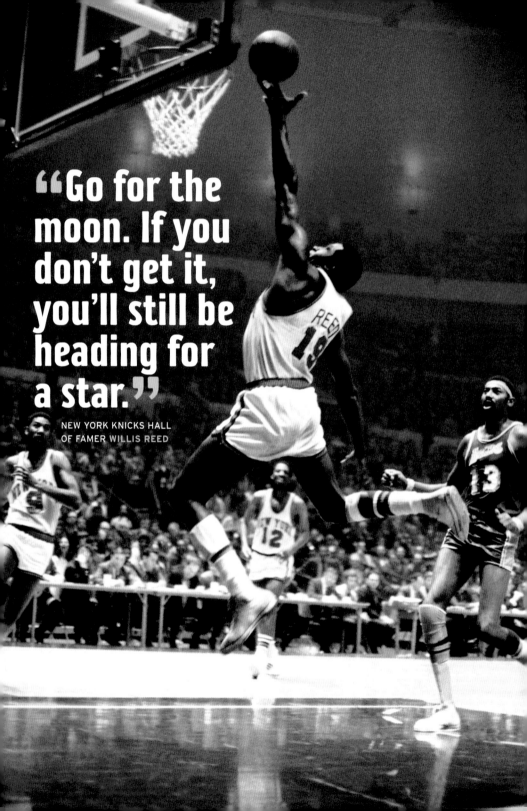

"Go for the moon. If you don't get it, you'll still be heading for a star."

NEW YORK KNICKS HALL OF FAMER WILLIS REED

"There are only two options regarding commitment. You're either *in* or you're *out*. There's no such thing as life in between."

MIAMI HEAT COACH **PAT RILEY**

"I've had enough success for two lifetimes. My success is talent put together with hard work and luck."

NBA HALL OF FAMER **KAREEM ABDUL-JABBAR**

"One day of practice is like one day of clean living. It doesn't do you any good."

LONGTIME NCAA BASKETBALL COACH **ABE LEMONS**

"I don't have the physical talent those guys have. My hard work has made me very good."

INDIANA PACERS STAR **REGGIE MILLER** ON WHY HE DIDN'T RATE HIMSELF AMONG MICHAEL JORDAN, SCOTTIE PIPPEN, GRANT HILL AND SHAQUILLE O'NEAL AS THE BEST PLAYERS IN THE NBA

"A lot of late nights in the gym, a lot of early mornings, especially when your friends are going out, you're going to the gym. Those are the sacrifices that you have to make if you want to be an NBA basketball player."

NEW JERSEY NETS STAR **JASON KIDD**

"I don't know if I practiced more than anybody, but I sure practiced enough. I still wonder if somebody — somewhere — was practicing more than me."

BOSTON CELTICS SUPERSTAR LARRY BIRD

"You can practice shooting eight hours a day, but if your technique is wrong, then all you become is very good at shooting the wrong way. Get the fundamentals down, and the level of everything you do will rise."

CHICAGO BULLS SUPERSTAR **MICHAEL JORDAN**

"Once you are labeled 'the best' you want to stay up there, and you can't do it by loafing around."

BOSTON CELTICS SUPERSTAR **LARRY BIRD**

" Excellence is the gradual result of always striving to do better."

MIAMI HEAT COACH **PAT RILEY**

"Nothing will work unless you do."

LEGENDARY UCLA COACH **JOHN WOODEN**

" **Good, better, best.**
Never let it rest.
Until your good is better and your
better is best. "

SAN ANTONIO SPURS STAR TIM DUNCAN

"I've got a theory that if you give 100 percent all of
the time, somehow things will work out in the end."

BOSTON CELTICS HALL OF FAMER LARRY BIRD

"If you don't do what's best for your body, you're the
one who comes up on the short end."

BASKETBALL SUPERSTAR JULIUS ERVING

"I always keep a ball in the car. You never know."

HOUSTON ROCKETS STAR HAKEEM OLAJUWON

"Is there any greater tribute in sport than the simple one of being a winner? Is there? This guy here is the greatest of them all."

LOS ANGELES LAKERS STAR JERRY WEST ON BOSTON CELTICS STAR BILL RUSSELL, WHOSE TEAM WON 11 NBA CHAMPIONSHIPS IN HIS 13 SEASONS

"After I played him for the first time, I said 'Let's see. He's four or five inches taller. He's 40 or 50 pounds heavier. His vertical leap is at least as good as mine. He can get up and down the floor as well as I can. And he's smart. The real problem with all this is I have to show up.'"

BOSTON CELTICS GREAT BILL RUSSELL ON FIRST FACING FELLOW NBA LEGEND WILT CHAMBERLAIN

"The only word I can use to describe what it was like coaching Michael Jordan in the beginning is 'intimidating.' His skill level and competitiveness were unlike anything I had ever seen."

PHIL JACKSON ON GETTING HIS FIRST NBA COACHING JOB WITH THE CHICAGO BULLS IN 1989

"I used to think that Michael Jordan was the Babe Ruth of basketball. I have now come to believe that

Babe Ruth

was the

Michael Jordan of baseball."

CHICAGO BULLS OWNER JERRY REINSDORF

" In dealing with someone like Dennis, you have to realize that he is an individual, but also, as a member of a team, he has to stay within certain guidelines. The difficult part was getting other players not to take issue with the fact that Dennis was going to be late, maybe show up 10 minutes before a game instead of an hour-and-a-half like everybody else. But we worked it out. We had mature players, and, in Dennis, we had a guy who wanted to win. "

PHIL JACKSON ON COACHING THE CHICAGO BULLS' DENNIS RODMAN

"We cut him off and there was nowhere for him to go but out of bounds... It's still the greatest move I've ever seen in basketball, the all-time greatest."

LOS ANGELES LAKERS SUPERSTAR **MAGIC JOHNSON** RECALLS JULIUS ERVING'S LAYUP FROM BEHIND THE BASKET IN THE 1980 NBA FINALS

"Jib, jab, through the legs, fancy dancing. All the spins, twirls, trick shots, all that's Earl Monroe. They called him The Pearl because he was a gem."

HALL OF FAMER **ALEX ENGLISH** ON FELLOW NBA LEGEND EARL "THE PEARL" MONROE

"He could get points if you put him in a tin can and closed the lid."

HOUSTON ROCKETS GUARD **MIKE NEWLIN** ON TEAMMATE CALVIN MURPHY

"I didn't mean to destroy it. It was the power, the chocolate thunder. I could feel it surging through my body, fighting to get out. I had no control over it."

PHILADELPHIA 76ERS STAR **DARRYL DAWKINS'** EXPLANATION AFTER SHATTERING THE GLASS BACKBOARD DURING A GAME

"We all thought he was a movie-star player, but we found out he wears a hard hat. It's like finding a great orthopedic surgeon who can also operate a bulldozer."

LOS ANGELES LAKERS COACH **PAUL WESTHEAD** AFTER ROOKIE GUARD MAGIC JOHNSON FILLED IN AT CENTER FOR THE INJURED KAREEM ABDUL-JABBAR AND SCORED 42 POINTS WITH 15 REBOUNDS IN A 123-107 WIN OVER THE PHILADELPHIA 76ERS IN GAME SIX TO WIN THE 1980 NBA CHAMPIONSHIP

"I don't think there will ever be another 6-foot-9 point guard who smiles while he humiliates you."

LOS ANGELES LAKERS STAR **JAMES WORTHY** ON LONGTIME TEAMMATE MAGIC JOHNSON

"I learned to give him the ball."

LOS ANGELES LAKERS SUPERSTAR **MAGIC JOHNSON** WHEN ASKED WHAT HE LEARNED ABOUT THE GAME OF BASKET-BALL BY PLAYING WITH KAREEM ABDUL-JABBAR

"If I'm going to play against Abdul-Jabbar, I'd like to have a month's notice."

BOSTON CELTIC **JIM ARD**

"If I have a choice whether to do the show or throw a straight pass, and we're going to get the basket either way, I'm going to do the show."

BASKETBALL LEGEND "PISTOL" PETE MARAVICH

"They don't pay you a million dollars for two-hand chest passes."

HALL OF FAMER PETE MARAVICH

"A lot of guys I've played with are all-stars and MVP candidates, but they don't act like that. They act like least valuable players. Steve acts like a most valuable player every day."

PHOENIX SUNS GUARD RAJA BELL ON TEAMMATE STEVE NASH

"As far as carrying the torch for the years to come, I don't know. I just want to be the best basketball player I can be."

LOS ANGELES LAKERS STAR KOBE BRYANT

"When I dunk, I put something on it. I want the ball to hit the floor before I do."

BACKBOARDING-BREAKING DUNK-SUPERSTAR
DARRYL DAWKINS

"The future is yours, but thanks for letting us have it one more year."

SAN ANTONIO SPURS STAR TIM DUNCAN TO LEBRON JAMES
AFTER THE SPURS SWEPT THE CAVALIERS TO WIN THE 2007
NBA CHAMPIONSHIP

"**He's not intimidated by anyone. He has that**

swagger

that most of the great ones have."

CLEVELAND CAVALIERS COACH PAUL SILAS ON LEBRON JAMES

"I was blessed with a God-given talent, and my mother raised me the right way."

CLEVELAND CAVALIERS STAR LEBRON JAMES

"My heroes are and were my parents. I can't see having anyone else as my heroes."

CHICAGO BULLS SUPERSTAR MICHAEL JORDAN

"I'm not a role model. Just because I dunk a basketball doesn't mean I should raise your kids."

NBA STAR CHARLES BARKLEY

"It doesn't bother me. I was also my wife's second choice, and we've been married for 25 years."

UNIVERSITY OF OKLAHOMA COACH BILLY TUBBS EXPLAINS WHY IT DIDN'T BOTHER HIM THAT HE WAS THE TEAM'S SECOND CHOICE

"It's one thing to hear about it from your coach, but when your wife tells you it stinks, you tend to work on it."

13-YEAR NBA VETERAN ORLANDO WOOLRIDGE ON A DEFICIENCY IN HIS GAME

"Uh, yeah. I mean, it's tough to say,
woulda, shoulda, coulda,
ifs and buts
like candy
and nuts,
you know,
you never know.
This, that and
the other thing.
Who knows?
You know, there's a lot of what-ifs.
You know, my whole life is a lot of
what-ifs."

TORONTO RAPTOR MATT BONNER WHEN ASKED IF THE
TEAM RESENTED FORMER RAPTOR VINCE CARTER

"I can't really remember the names of the clubs that we went to."

LOS ANGELES LAKERS STAR **SHAQUILLE O'NEAL** IN ANSWER TO A QUESTION ABOUT WHETHER OR NOT HE VISITED THE PARTHENON WHILE IN GREECE

"That was my fault. I should have read it before it came out."

PHILADELPHIA 76ERS STAR **CHARLES BARKLEY** ON BEING MISQUOTED IN HIS AUTOBIOGRAPHY

"Shaq is not the man. He's the man because the NBA wants him to be the man, but before you can be the man, you've got to be the man."

NBA VETERAN **DENNIS RODMAN** DISCUSSES THE YOUNG SHAQUILLE O'NEAL

"I think we played hard, but it was a lackadaisical hard."

NEW JERSEY NETS GUARD **OTIS BIRDSONG** EXPLAINS A LOSS

"I've learned that there's a time when it's in the team's interest not to say anything, and in some instances not saying anything is really saying a lot. A lot of people understand what not saying anything means, so, in effect, not saying anything is really saying a lot."

OUTSPOKEN PORTLAND TRAIL BLAZERS STAR **BILL WALTON**

"It's almost as if we have ESPN."

LOS ANGELES LAKERS SUPERSTAR **MAGIC JOHNSON** ON
PLAYING WITH JAMES WORTHY

"I am an equal-opportunity hater."

TORONTO RAPTORS COACH **SAM MITCHELL**

"I don't have the first clue who he is talking about because all I worry about is Jerome."

SEATTLE SUPERSONICS CENTER **JEROME JAMES** AFTER
COACH NATE McMILLAN CHARGED THAT HE WAS SELFISH

"It's my birthday. I was born on the 53rd of November."

NBA STAR **DARRYL DAWKINS** ON WHY HE WORE NUMBER 53
WITH THE PHILADELPHIA 76ERS AND NEW JERSEY NETS

"He's not fired. He's just not rehired."

BUFFALO BRAVES PR DIRECTOR **MIKE SHURE** ON THE
DECISION TO CUT TIES WITH COACH JACK RAMSAY

"**If it ain't broke, don't break it.**"

19-YEAR NBA VETERAN CHARLES OAKLEY

"It's not how good you can play when you play good. It's how good you play when you play bad, and we can play bad as good as anyone in the country."

UNIVERSITY OF GEORGIA COACH HUGH DURHAM

"Up and down."

HOUSTON ROCKETS GUARD VERNON MAXWELL, WHEN ASKED BY COACH DON CHANEY TO GIVE A ONE-WORD DESCRIPTION OF HIS SEASON

"Left hand, right hand, it doesn't matter. I'm amphibious."

NBA JOURNEYMAN CHARLES SHACKLEFORD

"Any time Detroit scores more than a hundred points and holds the other team below a hundred points they almost always win."

DETROIT PISTONS COACH DOUG COLLINS

"It's not going to be

peaches

and

gravy

all the time."

INDIANA PACERS CENTER **BRAD MILLER** ON HIS TEAM'S
STRUGGLES

"The rule was 'No autopsy, no foul.' "

CLEVELAND CAVALIERS ROOKIE **STEWART GRANGER** ON
THE PICKUP GAMES OF HIS BROOKLYN CHILDHOOD

"It only hurts when I'm on the bench."

LONG BEACH STATE FRESHMAN GUARD **DONNIE MARTIN**
ON HIS INJURED SHOULDER

"I sight down my nose to shoot, and now my nose
isn't straight since I broke it."

CENTENARY COLLEGE PLAYER **BARRIE HAYNIE** EXPLAINS
HIS SHOOTING WOES

" I threw my arms up and one just kept going. "

HOW CLEMSON UNIVERSITY COACH **BILL FOSTER**
DISLOCATED HIS SHOULDER DURING AN UPSET VICTORY

"You scored one more point than a dead man."

LONGTIME NCAA BASKETBALL COACH **ABE LEMONS** TO A
PLAYER WHO SCORED ONLY ONE POINT DESPITE PLAYING
MOST OF THE GAME

"With the way you dress, you must be blind."

SOUTHERN METHODIST UNIVERSITY POINT GUARD **BUTCH
MOORE** TELLS COACH DAVE BLISS WHY HE'D NICKNAMED
HIM "STEVIE" AFTER STEVIE WONDER

"I didn't know he was that ugly. I thought he was a
pretty good-looking fella when he had hair, but, oh
my goodness, did that bring out all his bad features
or what? He's going to be single all the rest of his life!"

DALLAS MAVERICKS COACH **DON NELSON** ON DIRK NOWITZKI'S
CREW CUT

"We have a great bunch of outside shooters.
Unfortunately, all our games are played indoors."

NEW MEXICO STATE COACH **WELDON DREW**

"What do you have when you have an agent buried
up to his neck in sand? Not enough sand."

ORLANDO MAGIC GENERAL MANAGER **PAT WILLIAMS**

"I don't care what people think. **People are stupid.**"

"When we play the game like we're supposed to play it, it is pretty easy. Making the extra pass, making the simple play. It's not about between your legs, behind your back and all of that – it's just about scoring the bucket."

UTAH JAZZ SUPERSTAR KARL MALONE

" Keep it simple.
When you get too complex,
you forget the obvious. "

MARQUETTE UNIVERSITY COACH AL McGUIRE

"You could tell five guys to go over to the post office at 2 o'clock and one of 'em wouldn't be there, so why have so many trick plays?"

OKLAHOMA CITY UNIVERSITY BASKETBALL COACH
ABE LEMONS ON HIS STRATEGY OF KEEPING THINGS SIMPLE

"My sister's expecting a baby, and I don't know if I'm going to be an uncle or an aunt."

NORTH CAROLINA STATE CENTER CHUCK NEVITT
EXPLAINING TO COACH JIM VALVANO WHY HE LOOKED
NERVOUS DURING A PRACTICE

"I'm expecting. We'll, I'm not. That would be weird."

CLEVELAND CAVALIERS STAR LEBRON JAMES, WHOSE
GIRLFRIEND WAS DUE TO DELIVER HIS SECOND SON

"It better taste good."

SAN ANTONIO SPURS TEAMMATE AND PARTY GUEST
MATT BONNER ON THE CAKE THAT REPORTEDLY COST
MORE THAN $33,000 FOR THE WEDDING OF TONY PARKER
TO *DESPERATE HOUSEWIVES* ACTRESS EVA LONGORIA

"You know what happened yesterday? Elton John [turned] 60 years old. He celebrated by having his 60th concert at Madison Square Garden. And then he beat the Knicks 102–94."

LATE NIGHT TALK SHOW HOST DAVID LETTERMAN

"All those little guys kept hitting my hands. And one guy kept running underneath me."

UNIVERSITY OF HOUSTON 7-FOOT CENTER **HAKEEM OLAJUWON** EXPLAINS HIS POOR PERFORMANCE IN THE FIRST HALF AGAINST SMALL-COLLEGE UNDERDOGS ST. MARY'S OF TEXAS

" He's America. Tomorrow, every father and son will be out in the driveway trying to dunk. If Spud can do it, anyone can. People will be talking about him on their way to work or riding the bus."

ATLANTA HAWKS HEAD COACH **MIKE FRATELLO** ON 5-FOOT-7 GUARD SPUD WEBB WINNING THE 1986 ALL-STAR SLAM DUNK CONTEST

"He has to wear low-cuts. The high-tops go over his knees."

A BOSTON CELTICS TV ANNOUNCER ON THE FOOTWEAR CHOICE OF 5-FOOT-3 **MUGGSY BOGUES** OF THE CHARLOTTE HORNETS

"The closer I got, the taller he looked."

PRO TENNIS PLAYER **EDDIE DIBBS**, WHO STOOD 5-FOOT-7, ON WHY HE TURNED DOWN THE CHANCE TO PLAY ONE-ON-ONE WITH 6-FOOT-10 NBA STAR BOB McADOO

"My father was an undertaker. There are advantages. For instance, while I was dating my wife, I sent her flowers every day."

LONGTIME NOTRE DAME COACH DIGGER PHELPS

"I couldn't shoot when I played so I teach defense."

MARQUETTE COACH AL McGUIRE EXPLAINS WHY HIS TEAMS
WERE INVOLVED IN SO MANY LOW-SCORING GAMES

"The only good thing about it was, if there were any recruits looking in, they know we need help."

UNIVERSITY OF HOUSTON COACH GUY LEWIS AFTER
A 23-POINT LOSS

"I just wanted to see what it feels like to be on the winning side. I'd forgotten."

WHY CAL STATE LOS ANGELES COACH NOB SCOTT SAT
DOWN ON THE OTHER TEAM'S BENCH DURING HIS TEAM'S
NINTH CONSECUTIVE LOSS

"There were enough bad passes and missed free throws to knock out any theories about coaching being responsible."

BOSTON CELTICS COACH BILL FITCH AFTER A GAME SEVEN
PLAYOFF LOSS TO THE PHILADELPHIA 76ERS

"When it comes to stitches and bruises, I've definitely been in the Christmas spirit in my career. I give more than I receive."

DALLAS MAVERICKS CENTER SHAWN BRADLEY

"We got in the Christmas spirit in the first half. At halftime I said, 'Bah, humbug.'"

CLEVELAND CAVALIERS COACH BILL FITCH EXPLAINING WHY HIS TEAM RALLIED TO BEAT THE BUFFALO BRAVES IN A CHRISTMAS DAY GAME

"I didn't think Christmas would ever come. When it did, I didn't give a dang. We were in Cincinnati."

LONGTIME NBA COACH DICK MOTTA ON HIS STRUGGLES DURING HIS FIRST YEAR IN THE LEAGUE

"When we were playing the Celtics once around Christmastime, Larry Bird pulled up for a three right in front of our bench and said, 'Merry Christmas.'"

TRASH-TALKING INDIANA PACERS STAR **REGGIE MILLER** ON THE BEST THING HE'D HEARD SOMEONE ELSE SAY ON THE COURT

"I'm tired of hearing about money, money, money, money, money. I just want to play the game, drink Pepsi, wear Reebok."

LOS ANGELES LAKERS STAR SHAQUILLE O'NEAL

"If I weren't earning **$3 million** a year to dunk a basketball, most people on the street would run in the other **direction** if they saw me coming."

PHILADELPHIA 76ERS STAR CHARLES BARKLEY

"Everything's great until we start playing, and you guys start telling me I'm not worth the money."

TORONTO RAPTORS COACH SAM MITCHELL TO THE MEDIA IN THE OFF-SEASON SHORTLY AFTER SIGNING A NEW FOUR-YEAR $16-MILLION CONTRACT

"I really don't like talking about money. All I can say is that the Good Lord must have wanted me to have it."

BOSTON CELTICS SUPERSTAR LARRY BIRD

"I didn't miss the smell of the gym, the bounce of the ball or the kids. I just ran out of money."

MISSISSIPPI STATE UNIVERSITY COACH BOB BOYD EXPLAINS HIS DECISION TO RETURN AFTER A TWO-YEAR RETIREMENT

"You're beautiful to me, baby. As long as that check comes on the 15th and 30th, you're gorgeous."

TORONTO RAPTORS COACH SAM MITCHELL AFTER TEASING THE TEAM'S DIRECTOR OF BASKETBALL FINANCE FOR WEARING A BANDANA

"I was thinking I was going to be a rich man until the government stepped in and took it all."

AUSTRALIAN-BORN LUC LONGLEY ON NBA SALARIES AND U.S. TAXES

"We might make a lot of money, but we also spend a lot of money."

NEW YORK KNICKS STAR PATRICK EWING

"I never thought I wouldn't make it. I never felt I would give up or work a nine-to-five."

27-YEAR-OLD TORONTO RAPTORS ROOKIE **JAMARIO MOON**, WHO SPENT SIX YEARS WITH 18 TEAMS IN EIGHT LEAGUES BEFORE EVEN ATTENDING HIS FIRST NBA TRAINING CAMP

"A nine-to-five job, I don't know – my father tells me I'm too lazy. I put more effort into basketball than anything else. A nine-to-five job, I won't be able to wake up. Basketball motivates me to wake up every morning."

HOFSTRA UNIVERSITY GUARD AND TOP SCORER **ANTOINE AGUDIO** ON HOW LAZINESS MOTIVATES HIM TO WORK SO HARD

"Sport is the only profession I know of that, when you retire, you have to go to work."

NBA HALL OF FAMER **EARL "THE PEARL" MONROE**

"I can't imagine working nine-to-five.
I think that would

suck."

NBA STAR TURNED BROADCASTER CHARLES BARKLEY

"I got tired of doing nothing."

LONGTIME NCAA AND WNBA COACH VAN CHANCELLOR ON WHY HE CAME OUT OF RETIREMENT (AND GAVE UP PLAYING GOLF) TO TAKE THE JOB COACHING THE WOMEN'S BASKET-BALL TEAM AT LOUISIANA STATE UNIVERSITY

"I've worked all my life, but I've had a job that I didn't think was a job. In other words, I never have thought I had a job. I just loved what I was doing. I made no money for a ton of years but I still loved it. I never did get up in the morning and say I was going to work."

LONGTIME WOMEN'S COACH VAN CHANCELLOR

"You've got to follow every lead. You've got to see everybody. And you've got to get lucky... But it sure beats work."

80-YEAR-OLD NBA SCOUTING DIRECTOR MARTY BLAKE ON THE LIFE OF A SCOUT

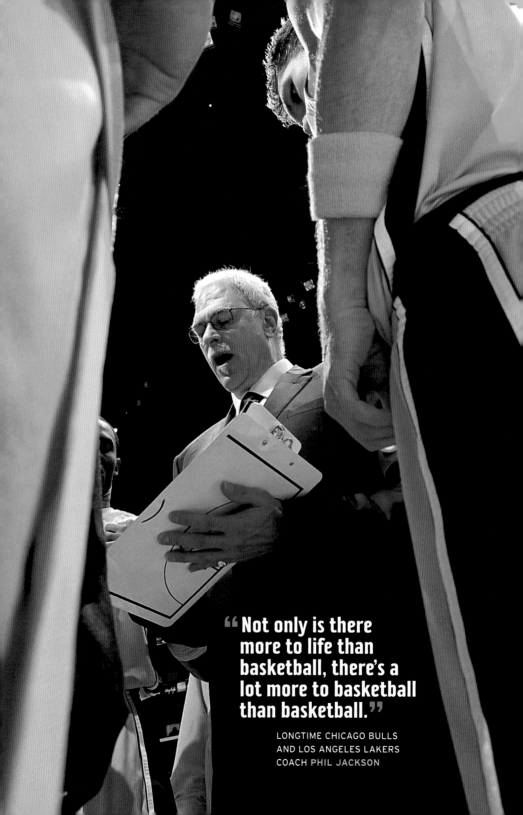

"Not only is there more to life than basketball, there's a lot more to basketball than basketball."

LONGTIME CHICAGO BULLS AND LOS ANGELES LAKERS COACH PHIL JACKSON

"If you make every game a life and death proposition, you're going to have problems. For one thing, you'll be dead a lot."

UNIVERSITY OF NORTH CAROLINA COACHING LEGEND
DEAN SMITH

"You don't play against opponents. You play against the game of basketball."

LEGENDARY NCAA COACH BOBBY KNIGHT

"If you fall into a puddle wearing a new suit, you can either whine for months about ruining your suit or check for fish."

CANADIAN NATIONAL TEAM COACH JACK DONOHUE

"Basketball is like photography, if you don't focus, all you have is the negative."

DAN FRISBY

"Just because there's glass on the road don't mean there's been an accident."

19-YEAR NBA VETERAN CHARLES OAKLEY

"Do I feel tested? Yeah. I'll either pass or fail. That's why they call it a test."

MIAMI HEAT STAR SHAQUILLE O'NEAL, BATTLING INJURIES
AND A SCORING SLUMP DURING THE 2007-08 SEASON, AND
THE OPINION OF MANY THAT HE MAY BE FINISHED AT AGE 35

"The strong take from the smart take

weak, and **the from the strong."**

PRINCETON BASKETBALL COACH **PETE CARRIL**

"It's a lot, and you try to live up to all of it. But, really, all you've got to do is go out there and play basketball."

OHIO STATE STAR GREG ODEN ON THE PRESSURE OF BEING PICKED FIRST OVERALL IN THE 2007 NBA DRAFT

"Nobody played the way we did. If they did, we wouldn't have won so many championships."

BOSTON CELTICS LEGEND BILL RUSSELL

"They said playing basketball would kill me. Well, not playing basketball was killing me."

LOS ANGELES LAKERS STAR MAGIC JOHNSON ON HIS COMEBACK FROM RETIREMENT AFTER BEING DIAGNOSED HIV POSITIVE

"I'm not comfortable being preachy, but more people need to start spending as much time in the library as they do on the basketball court."

NBA LEGEND KAREEM ABDUL-JABBAR

"We've really got nobody who's trying to be out there in the spotlight every single night."

DETROIT PISTONS GUARD CHAUNCEY BILLUPS ON HIS VETERAN TEAM'S SUCCESSFUL NO-NONSENSE APPROACH

"That and a dollar leaves you with a dollar."

MAVERICKS OWNER MARK CUBAN ON DALLAS BEING THE BEST TEAM DURING THE 2006-07 REGULAR SEASON. (THE MAVS WERE UPSET IN THE FIRST ROUND OF THE PLAYOFFS)

"People say I enjoy being famous. I don't. But what choice do I have?"

NBA LEGEND AND TV COMMENTATOR **CHARLES BARKLEY**

"I know you get pissed off hearing it, you get pissed off with me saying it, you get pissed off with the media saying it. But guess what, we're all going to keep saying it until you get better at it."

TORONTO RAPTORS COACH **SAM MITCHELL** TELLS SECOND-YEAR CENTER ANDREA BARGNANI ABOUT THE NEED TO IMPROVE HIS REBOUNDING AND PHYSICAL PLAY

"I don't like the Big Three. You have to win first, and then you can be called Big something."

BOSTON CELTICS COACH **DOC RIVERS** ON THE MEDIA TAG PUT ON PAUL PIERCE AND THE NEWLY ACQUIRED RAY ALLEN AND KEVIN GARNETT BEFORE THE 2007-08 SEASON

"You shut all that up by just trying to win ball games. You win – and you have nothing to talk about."

CLEVELAND CAVALIERS STAR **LEBRON JAMES** ON CRITICISM THAT HE IS TOO SELFLESS TO BE A TRUE SUPERSTAR

"I don't know if people truly understand how hard it is."

UNIVERSITY OF FLORIDA COACH **BILLY DONOVAN**, WHEN ASKED ABOUT HIS TEAM'S CHANCES OF REPEATING AS NCAA CHAMPIONS IN 2007. (THEY DID)

"Once I grew from 6 feet 1 to about 6 feet 6, by that time I was going into 12th grade, and that's when I started wanting to play basketball because, pretty much, basketball players always got the girl."

NBA JOURNEYMAN ERIC WILLIAMS

"If you're in this tournament long enough, you're going to go down."

DUKE UNIVERSITY COACH MIKE KRZYZEWSKI AFTER HIS TEAM LOST TO VIRGINIA COMMONWEALTH IN THE FIRST ROUND OF THE 2007 NCAA TOURNAMENT

" The secret is to have eight great players, and four others who will cheer like crazy. "

UNLV COACH JERRY TARKANIAN ON WINNING

"The main ingredient of stardom is the rest of the team."

CELEBRATED UCLA COACH JOHN WOODEN

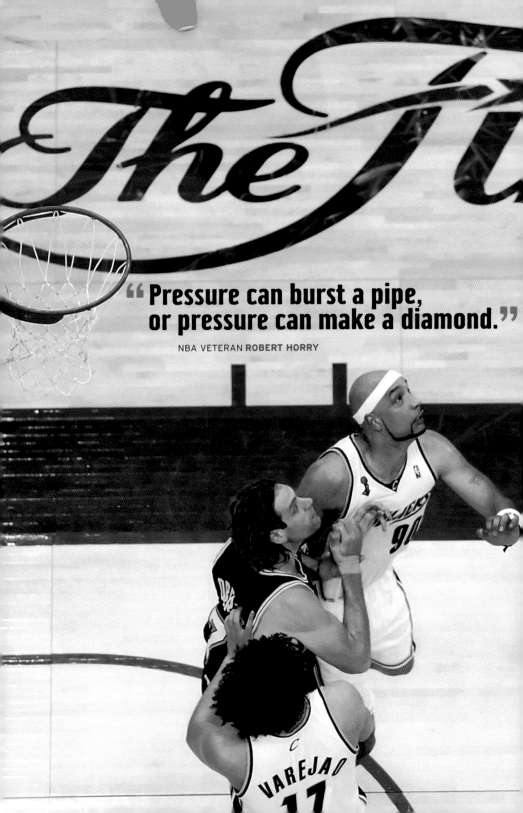

"Pressure can burst a pipe,
or pressure can make a diamond."

NBA VETERAN **ROBERT HORRY**

"I never looked at the consequences of missing a big shot... When you think about the consequences, you always think of a negative result."

CHICAGO BULLS SUPERSTAR MICHAEL JORDAN

"I don't get nervous in any situation. There's no such thing as nerves when you're playing games."

NBA SUPERSTAR SHAQUILLE O'NEAL

" I'm not afraid of nothing, I just like the challenge, and I love being here. "

CLEVELAND CAVALIERS STAR LEBRON JAMES

"I've always considered myself a crunch-time player. I just love having the ball in my hands. Everyone in the arena knows the ball is supposed to be in your hands, and you still make it. It's the odds. I love the odds."

INDIANA PACERS STAR REGGIE MILLER AFTER SCORING EIGHT POINTS IN THE FINAL 8.9 SECONDS IN A 1995 PLAYOFF VICTORY OVER THE NEW YORK KNICKS

"You can say something to popes, kings and presidents, but you can't talk to officials. In the next war, they ought to give everybody a whistle."

UNIVERSITY OF TEXAS COACH **ABE LEMONS**

"I wanted to have a career in sports when I was young, but I had to give it up. I'm only 6 feet tall, so I couldn't play basketball. I'm only 190 pounds, so I couldn't play football. And I have 20-20 vision, so I couldn't be a referee."

TONIGHT SHOW HOST **JAY LENO**

"Officiating is the only occupation in the world where the highest accolade is silence."

NBA REFEREE **EARL STROM**

"The first thing to remember is never to say, 'You're out!' "

BASKETBALL OFFICIAL **AL ROSSI** ON HIS ADVICE TO YOUNG REFEREES

"I told the NBA people I was only available on days ending in Y."

EASTERN LEAGUE REFEREE **ROGER McCANN** AFTER BEING PRESSED INTO EMERGENCY SERVICE FOR AN NBA GAME

" **I don't count 'em, I just call 'em.** "

NBA REFEREE EARL STROM ANSWERING COMPLAINTS THAT HE WAS CALLING TOO MANY FOULS AGAINST THE COMPLAINING TEAM

"It's true the ACC is the top league in the country. When you leave a gym in the SEC or Metro 7, they pour beer on your head. In the ACC, they soak you with Jack Daniels."

NCAA REFEREE JACK MANTON

"I'm not going to say anything about the officiating because it might take two days."

IOWA STATE COACH JOHNNY ORR AFTER HIS TEAM GOT ONLY NINE FREE THROW ATTEMPTS TO HIS OPPONENTS' 35 IN A 73-70 LOSS TO MISSOURI

"The trouble with the officials is they just don't care who wins."

CENTENARY COLLEGE COACH TOMMY CANTERBURY

"I got a tech for looking at an official, got a tech for laughing, got a tech for saying, 'Ball don't lie.' Got a tech for shaking my head. Got a tech for saying, 'Bad call.' It really doesn't matter what I do."

DETROIT PISTON RASHEED WALLACE

"I liked the officials. They couldn't understand a word I was saying."

UNIVERSITY OF MARYLAND COACH LEFTY DRIESELL AFTER RETURNING FROM A SERIES OF INTERNATIONAL GAMES IN MEXICO

"Larry Bird just throws the ball in the air, and God moves the basket underneath it."

CLEVELAND CAVALIERS PUBLIC ADDRESS ANNOUNCER
HOWIE CHIZEK AFTER THE BOSTON STAR SET A CLUB
RECORD WITH 60 POINTS IN ONE GAME AND SCORED 48 IN
ANOTHER AGAINST THE CAVS DURING THE 1984-85 SEASON

"He is the most exciting, awesome player in the game today. I think it's just God disguised as Michael Jordan."

BOSTON CELTICS SUPERSTAR LARRY BIRD AFTER MICHAEL
JORDAN SCORED 63 POINTS AGAINST THE CELTICS IN A 1986
PLAYOFF GAME

" Man, meeting Michael Jordan for me was like Black Jesus walking towards me. It was overwhelming to me to finally meet the guy I've looked up to my whole life. "

CLEVELAND CAVALIERS STAR LEBRON JAMES

"If you meet the Buddha in the lane,

feed him the ball."

LONGTIME CHICAGO BULLS AND LOS ANGELES LAKERS COACH PHIL JACKSON

"I see they are calling us a team of destiny. I guess that means we're not a very good team. We play hard, we're tough and that's why we win. No one likes us. No one thought we should be here. But I'm not saying prayers. There aren't any old ladies going to churches making novenas for us to win. This team is good. That's why we're winning."

GOLDEN STATE WARRIORS COACH AL ATTLES CONSIDERS HIS 1975 NBA CHAMPIONS

"This isn't a religious happening. This isn't due to transcendental meditation working in some myste- rious way. This is us."

GOLDEN STATE WARRIORS STAR CHARLES JOHNSON ON THE TEAM'S 1975 TITLE

" The main thing to remember about Michael is that God only made one. "

CHICAGO BULLS ASSISTANT COACH JOHN BACH ON MICHAEL JORDAN

"It's really amazing to think that some kid out there is going to open a pack of basketball cards one day soon and see my face on one of them."

PORTLAND TRAILBLAZER **GREG ODEN**, THE FIRST CHOICE IN THE 2007 NBA DRAFT, LOOKS FORWARD TO HIS ROOKIE CARD

"Just to get to this point, every guy in here has had to work really hard on their game. When a kid out there gets my card, I want him to be excited about it."

SEATTLE SUPERSONIC **KEVIN DURANT**, THE SECOND CHOICE IN THE 2007 NBA DRAFT, ON HIS ROOKIE CARD

" I was big into rookie cards, and now I'm a part of my own collection, which is kind of weird."

MEMPHIS GRIZZLIE AND FOURTH OVERALL 2007 NBA DRAFT PICK **MIKE CONLEY JR.** ON HIS ROOKIE CARD

"I want to build a legacy like those players did. I want my card to make a kid's day and to maybe be worth something someday."

GOLDEN STATE WARRIOR **BRANDAN WRIGHT**, WHO USED TO HOPE TO GET THE CARDS OF PLAYERS LIKE MICHAEL JORDAN AND KEVIN GARNETT, ON HIS OWN NBA ROOKIE CARD

"He came here when he heard that A&M was an engineering school, but when he found out they wouldn't let him drive a train he quit."

TEXAS A&M COACH **SHELBY METCALF** REMEMBERS A PLAYER WHO LEFT THE TEAM

"One year I was like 'I need to go back and see how close I am to graduating.' I started adding up all my credits, and I asked the guy, 'What am I?' He says, 'You're a freshman.' "

NBA STAR TURNED BROADCASTER **CHARLES BARKLEY**

"Because my grandma said I have to."

PHILADELPHIA 76ERS STAR **CHARLES BARKLEY** ON WHY HE PLANNED TO RETURN TO AUBURN TO EARN CREDITS TOWARD HIS DEGREE DESPITE EARNING $2 MILLION A SEASON

"I can't miss class. The professor doesn't have to call the roll to know I'm not there."

NORTH CAROLINA STATE'S 7-FOOT-4 **TOM BURLESON**

"There was no place I could go to cut classes."

BOSTON CELTICS FORWARD **MARVIN BARNES** EXPLAINS WHY
HE MADE UP SO MANY COLLEGE CREDITS WHILE IN PRISON

" I don't know why people question the academic training of a student athlete. Half the doctors in the country graduated in the bottom half of their class. "

MARQUETTE COACH **AL McGUIRE**

"I didn't even know Oregon was a state."

OREGON DUCKS FRESHMAN GUARD **TAJUAN PORTER**, WHO
ADMITS HE KNEW LITTLE ABOUT OREGON UNTIL A TEAM-
MATE AT HIS DETROIT HIGH SCHOOL WAS RECRUITED TO
PLAY THERE

"No, but they gave me one anyway."

LOS ANGELES LAKERS FORWARD **ELDEN CAMPBELL**, WHEN
ASKED IF HE HAD EARNED HIS DEGREE FROM CLEMSON

"If I keep playing, my name will be inscripted in the NBA bible for many years to come."

NBA SUPERSTAR SHAQUILLE O'NEAL

"He's a little bit younger, he's got a lot of proving to do, but he's just as lethal. It's my job to make him lethaler. It's my job to make him the lethalest, if that's a word..."

SHAQUILLE O'NEAL DISCUSSES MIAMI HEAT TEAMMATE DWYANE WADE

"I know this kid was good, but he's gooder than I thought."

SHAQ ON DWYANE WADE

"They are that same group, but I've got my own rivalristic problems. Is that a word, rivalristic? I've got my own rivalristic problems in the Eastern Conference."

SHAQ ON THE SACRAMENTO KINGS, FORMER RIVALS WHEN HE WAS IN THE WESTERN CONFERENCE WITH THE LOS ANGELES LAKERS

"He awokened a sleeping giant. I know that's not a word."

SHAQ RESPONDS TO FORMER TEAMMATE MALIK ALLEN, WHO WAS PROVOKING HIM

"My prognostical prognosis, my assumption, I'll say about three weeks."

SHAQ PREDICTS WHEN DWYANE WADE WOULD BE READY TO RETURN AFTER OFF-SEASON KNEE SURGERY THAT DID NOT HAVE HIM READY TO START THE 2007-08 SEASON

"When it comes to ridiculization, if you can't walk in a man's shoes, you shouldn't ridicule him."

SHAQUILLE O'NEAL

"I'm a very quotatious person."

SHAQUILLE O'NEAL

"Baryshnikov was great, but the play needs a shot clock."

BASKETBALL COMMENTATOR BUCKY WATERS AFTER WATCHING MIKHAIL BARYSHNIKOV IN A SHOW BASED ON FRANZ KAFKA'S METAMORPHOSIS

"Me and Mickey Mouse will be here forever."

21-YEAR-OLD DWIGHT HOWARD, THE FIRST-OVERALL PICK IN THE 2004 NBA DRAFT, ON SIGNING A FIVE-YEAR CONTRACT EXTENSION WITH THE ORLANDO MAGIC IN 2007

"Omelets for dinner? This is the best day of my life!"

CLEVELAND CAVALIERS STAR LEBRON JAMES, GUEST VOICING ON THE SIMPSONS

"That was a good day too."

LEBRON AGAIN, AFTER LISA SIMPSON REMINDED HIM HE HAD JUST SIGNED A $90-MILLION CONTRACT

"The difference between those three is in *The Godfather* trilogy. One is Fredo, who was never ready for me to hand it over to him. One is Sonny, who will do whatever it takes to be the man. And one is Michael, who if you watch the trilogy, the Godfather hands it over to Michael. So I have no problem handing it over to Dwyane."

NBA SUPERSTAR SHAQUILLE O'NEAL ON HIS RELATIONSHIPS WITH PENNY HARDAWAY, KOBE BRYANT AND DWYANE WADE

"In my prime I could have handled Michael Jordan. Of course, he would be only 12 years old."

NBA PLAYER TURNED COACH JERRY SLOAN

"Winning is overrated. The only time it is really important is in surgery and war."

TV ANALYST AND FORMER MARQUETTE UNIVERSITY COACH AL McGUIRE

"The whole subject of repeating is already getting repetitive."

SAN ANTONIO SPURS GUARD BRENT BARRY AT TRAINING CAMP FOLLOWING THE TEAM'S 2007 NBA CHAMPIONSHIP

"He's not that good. It's all computer-generated."

CLEVELAND CAVALIER SCOTT POLLARD ON TEAMMATE LEBRON JAMES

"I thank my teammates for letting their men blow by them."

MIAMI HEAT CENTER ALONZO MOURNING, JOKING AFTER WINNING HIS SECOND STRAIGHT DEFENSIVE PLAYER OF THE YEAR AWARD IN 2000

"I've been here so long that when I got here, the Dead Sea wasn't even sick."

UNIVERSITY OF ALABAMA COACH WIMP SANDERSON ON LASTING 32 YEARS AT THE SCHOOL

"The towels were so fluffy I could hardly close my suitcase."

80-YEAR-OLD NBA SCOUTING DIRECTOR MARTY BLAKE ON THE TITLE HE'S SELECTED FOR HIS LONG-AWAITED MEMOIR

"If that guy makes a turnover, we're gonna be in deep trouble."

FORMER DALLAS MAVERICKS EXECUTIVE RICK SUND ON A HALFTIME SHOW FEATURING A MAN JUGGLING CHAINSAWS

"Sorry, but I aimed for the basket in the middle."

SEATTLE SUPERSONICS GUARD BILL HANZLIK EXPLAINS TO COACH LENNY WILKINS WHY HE MISSED BOTH FREE THROWS AFTER BEING KNOCKED DIZZY ON A FOUL

" I was just getting acquainted with the wood. I wanted to see if it was maple or pine. "

LOS ANGELES LAKERS FORWARD KURT RAMBIS AFTER BEING KICKED IN THE HEAD, KNOCKED TO THE FLOOR AND SHOVED OUT OF BOUNDS

"**It was like *Hamlet*.**
Suspense,
a thriller
and then I killed them."

PHOENIX SUN QUENTIN RICHARDSON RECALLS A GAME-
WINNING SHOT

"Now that I'm in Detroit I'd like to change my name to
Abdul Automobile."

DETROIT PISTONS FORWARD M.L. CARR

"Tom."

NEWLY HIRED HOUSTON ROCKETS COACH TOM NISSALKE,
WHEN ASKED HOW TO PRONOUNCE HIS NAME

"Don't you ever pass?"

NBA LEGEND BOB COUSY AFTER TEAMMATE BILL SHARMAN'S
LENGTH-OF-THE-COURT ATTEMPTED PASS TO HIM SWISHED
THROUGH THE NET FOR A BASKET DURING THE 1957 NBA
ALL-STAR GAME

"I wasn't aware I had a perfect night."

PHOENIX SUN CENTER DENNIS AWTREY AFTER FINDING OUT
HE'D BEEN 0-FOR-7 FROM THE FLOOR

"If I'm going to be unhappy, I might as well be unhappy where it's warm."

ARIZONA STATE'S RICKER McCUTHEON, WHO HAD
TRANSFERRED FROM THE UNIVERSITY OF MINNESOTA
BECAUSE OF A DIFFICULT TEAM SITUATION

"I'd rather be a football coach. That way you can lose only 11 games a season. I lost 11 games in December alone."

PAN AMERICAN COLLEGE COACH ABE LEMONS

"All it means is I get to shake hands with guys I already know."

NBA LEGEND JERRY WEST ON BEING NAMED CAPTAIN OF THE LOS ANGELES LAKERS

"I probably would have broken my ankle."

CLEVELAND CAVALIERS STAR LEBRON JAMES, WHO TWISTED HIS ANKLE BADLY WHILE WEARING NEW SHOES IN HIS SPONSOR'S LINE, ON WHAT WOULD HAVE HAPPENED IF HE HAD BEEN WEARING ANOTHER COMPANY'S SHOES

"Too bad he wasn't 40."

SPRINGFIELD COLLEGE COACH ED BILIK AFTER FORWARD IVAN OLIVARES SCORED 24 POINTS ON HIS 24TH BIRTHDAY

"Kids are great. That's one of the best things about our business, all the kids you get to meet. It's a shame they have to grow up to be regular people and come to the games and call you names."

NBA STAR CHARLES BARKLEY

"We had a lot of nicknames —

Scarface, Blackie, Toothless

— and those were just the cheerleaders."

UTAH JAZZ COACH **FRANK LAYDEN** REMEMBERS HIS HIGH SCHOOL DAYS IN BROOKLYN

"If I could look into the future, I wouldn't be sitting here talking to you doorknobs. I'd be out investing in the stock market."

BOSTON CELTICS GREAT KEVIN McHALE, WHEN ASKED TO ASSESS HIS TEAM'S PROSPECTS IN AN UPCOMING SEASON

"You don't elbow the King. If you elbow the King, they throw you in the dungeon."

LOS ANGELES LAKERS BACKUP CENTER MYCHAL THOMPSON, WHEN ASKED WHY HE DIDN'T RESPOND AFTER KAREEM ABDUL-JABBAR HIT HIM WITH AN ELBOW DURING PRACTICE

"I've learned I can't help the team sitting on the bench."

NBA LEGEND WILT CHAMBERLAIN EXPLAINING WHY HE NEVER FOULED OUT

"I don't think we would have won that game if we didn't have the plane."

SACRAMENTO KINGS COACH DICK MOTTA JUSTIFIES THE EXPENSE OF A PRIVATE PLANE AFTER THE TEAM WENT 1-40 ON THE ROAD

"If we stay free of injuries, we'll be in contention to be a healthy team."

NEW JERSEY NET CHRIS MORRIS, WHEN ASKED ABOUT HIS TEAM'S CHANCES IN 1993

"**Dealing with the press.
After the demands
of a game, my mind
needs a rest.**"

INDIANA UNIVERSITY COACH BOBBY KNIGHT'S
FAVORITE PART OF THE JOB

"He looks like he went to the blood bank and forgot to say when."

PHILADELPHIA 76ERS GENERAL MANAGER **PAT WILLIAMS**, WHEN ASKED ABOUT THE 7-FOOT-7 BUT RAIL-THIN MANUTE BOL

"You mean in the state?"

UNIVERSITY OF TEXAS COACH **ABE LEMONS**, WHEN ASKED IF HE THOUGHT HIS TEAM SHOULD BE RANKED IN THE TOP 10

"I've never heard of a plane that backed into a mountain."

VANDERBILT COACH **C.M. NEWTON** EXPLAINS HIS HABIT OF SITTING IN THE LAST SEAT ON TEAM FLIGHTS

"I hate it. It looks like a stickup at a 7-Eleven. Five guys standing there with their hands in the air."

LONGTIME NCAA COACH **NORM SLOAN** DESCRIBES ZONE DEFENSE

"I guess there's not a lot of sun in gyms."

UCLA FORWARD **KIKI VANDEWEGHE**, WHEN ASKED BY AN EAST COAST WRITER WHY HE DIDN'T HAVE A TAN

"When you're in a complete state of panic, you can't move."

SEATTLE SUPERSONICS COACH **BILL RUSSELL** EXPLAINS WHY HE DIDN'T DO ANYTHING AS THE NEW JERSEY NETS JUMPED OUT TO A 17-0 LEAD IN THE GAME'S FIRST SEVEN MINUTES

"Dynasties get better as they get older. After a while they begin to win games not so much on talent as on the confidence that comes with experience. They succeed because they know they have succeeded in the past. If you don't develop that ability, you cannot become a team that becomes a repeat champion."

LOS ANGELES LAKERS COACH PAT RILEY

"I'd rather have a lot of talent and a little experience than a lot of experience and a little talent."

LEGENDARY UCLA COACH JOHN WOODEN

"The difference, you know, between all the teams in this league is very slight. All you need is an edge. When the game starts there are 10 guys out there just looking for an edge. That's why one team can win by 20 points and then turn around and get beat by the same team by 20 points – losing the edge."

BOSTON CELTICS LEGEND BILL RUSSELL

"Concentration and mental toughness are the margins of victory."

NBA HALL OF FAMER AND COACH BILL RUSSELL

"When you get to that level, it's not a matter of talent anymore — because all the players are so talented — it's about preparation, about playing smart and making good decisions."

HOUSTON ROCKETS STAR HAKEEM OLAJUWON

"When things don't go well, we look to him all the time to make the tough play. We probably do it too much. Sometimes I'll have an open shot and still pass to him, even though he's farther out and two guys are on him. We do this instinctively because he has usually been the guy who's turned bad moments into good ones for us."

BOSTON CELTICS STAR PAUL SILAS ON TEAM LEADER JOHN HAVLICEK

"One man can be a crucial ingredient on a team, but one man cannot make a team."

BASKETBALL LEGEND KAREEM ABDUL-JABBAR

"Ask not what your teammates can do for you. Ask what you can do for your teammates."

LOS ANGELES LAKERS STAR MAGIC JOHNSON

"I'd much rather be second fiddle on a contender than a so-called superstar on a bad team."

DETROIT PISTON RICHARD HAMILTON

"Team has to come first. You have to care about each other more than you care about yourself. If you care about the guy to your left and the guy to your right more than you care about yourself, you know who's going to get taken care of? The guy in the middle."

TORONTO RAPTORS COACH **SAM MITCHELL**

"On every sports team there are conflicts. Pro teams are made of conflicts. It is their nature; we are all competing. Why we succeed is because, on the Knicks, our conflicts never turn to bitterness."

NEW YORK KNICKS STAR (AND FUTURE U.S. SENATOR) **BILL BRADLEY**

"Sometimes a player's greatest challenge is coming to grips with his role on the team."

CHICAGO BULLS STAR **SCOTTIE PIPPEN**

"In New York, you're either dead or alive. You lose a game and you're dead, and you win one and you basically get to survive. So you don't necessarily relax and say it's over. If we don't win Monday, then it's the same thing all over again."

NEW YORK KNICKS COACH ISAIAH THOMAS AFTER THE KNICKS SNAPPED AN EIGHT-GAME LOSING STREAK EARLY IN THE 2007–08 SEASON

"When it's the middle of January and the sun is shining and it's beautiful outside, who wants to come inside and watch the Lakers lose?"

NBA SUPERSTAR KAREEM ABDUL-JABBAR ON THE TEAM'S DIFFICULTIES IN HIS EARLY LAKERS DAYS, AFTER COMING OVER FROM THE MILWAUKEE BUCKS

"We're not a very good basketball team right now. This is very disappointing. We couldn't hit a bull in the butt with a bass fiddle."

INDIANA PACERS COACH RICK CARLISLE

"Coach told us, 'Don't get into a track meet.' We got into a track meet with Marion Jones and Carl Lewis – and we're running like Bill Cosby."

UTAH JAZZ FORWARD OLDEN POLYNICE AFTER A 107-77 BLOWOUT BY THE DALLAS MAVERICKS

"We suck in practice too."

PHILADELPHIA 76ERS FORWARD ANDRE IGUODALA
ON THE TEAM'S STRUGGLES DURING THE FIRST HALF
OF THE 2007–08 SEASON

"What's the risk? That we play worse? We can't play much worse than we did in Games 3 and 4, so you've got to try something."

RAPTORS COACH **SAM MITCHELL**, WHOSE THIRD DIFFERENT STARTING LINEUP IN AS MANY GAMES KEPT TORONTO ALIVE IN ITS 2007 PLAYOFF SERIES WITH NEW JERSEY

"The guy has been great, but today? Forget the shooting — anybody is going to have a day like that — but some of the passes? We actually had point-shaving allegations in our locker room after the game."

ORLANDO MAGIC COACH **STU VAN GUNDY** JOKES AFTER HIDAYET TURKOGLU TURNED THE BALL OVER SEVEN TIMES BUT THEN HIT THE GAME-WINNING SHOT WITH 0.7 SECONDS REMAINING IN A 112-110 OVERTIME WIN OVER THE CHICAGO BULLS

"I know we're making some mistakes because we're young, but every once in a while we play as wild as dirt-road lizards."

MISSISSIPPI STATE COACH **KERMIT DAVIS** ON HIS TEAM'S PROBLEM WITH TURNOVERS

"It's so bad that the players are giving each other high fives when they hit the rim."

SOUTHEASTERN MISSOURI UNIVERSITY COACH **RON SHUMATEON** ON HIS TEAM'S POOR SHOOTING

"We just dug ourselves a 10-foot hole then dug out 9 feet, 11 inches."

ORAL ROBERTS UNIVERSITY COACH KEN HAYES ON LOSING
TO OKLAHOMA STATE BY TWO POINTS AFTER TRAILING BY 13
AT HALFTIME

"Fans never fall asleep at our games because they're afraid they might get hit by a pass."

LONGTIME NCAA COACH GEORGE RAVELING

"The way we're playing, it doesn't matter who comes back. Jesus Christ could come back, and we still wouldn't have a chance."

LOS ANGELES LAKERS COACH PHIL JACKSON AFTER A
BLOWOUT LOSS TO THE DALLAS MAVERICKS

"They're a good defensive team ... but we missed dunks, we missed layups, we missed free throws. We did everything you need to do to win the game. The ball just didn't go in the hole."

RUTGERS UNIVERSITY COACH FRED HILL AFTER A 58-46
LOSS TO GEORGETOWN

"Things got so bad that I had to play my student manager for a while. They got really bad when she started to complain to the press that she wasn't getting enough playing time."

UNIVERSITY OF MINNESOTA WOMEN'S BASKETBALL COACH
LINDA HILL-McDONALD

"We were afraid we'd get arrested for impersonating a basketball team."

TULANE COACH **ROY DANFORTH** ON WHY HIS TEAM GOT
OUT OF PHILADELPHIA SO FAST AFTER A LOSS TO PENN

"A tough day at the office is even tougher when your office contains spectator seating."

NEW ZEALAND BASKETBALL COACH **NIK POSA**

"I've been watching you guys and you made me sick."

SACRAMENTO KINGS ASSISTANT COACH (AND FORMER NBA
STAR) **WILLIS REED** TELLS PLAYERS WHY HE WAS FEELING ILL

"I guess it's business before loyalty. But, wow. He said that?"

> FORMER LOS ANGELES LAKERS STAR **SHAQUILLE O'NEAL**
> AFTER LEARNING THAT LAKERS OWNER JERRY BUSS SAID
> HE WOULD CONSIDER DEALING KOBE BRYANT, WHO HAD
> REQUESTED A TRADE PRIOR TO THE 2007-08 SEASON

"I've read over the years that I was as much a Bay Area landmark as the Golden Gate Bridge. But I'm going and that bridge isn't going anywhere."

> LONGTIME GOLDEN STATE WARRIORS CENTER **NATE THURMOND**
> AFTER BEING TRADED TO THE CHICAGO BULLS

"They all want to give me bad players, and I've got enough of those."

> ATLANTA HAWKS GENERAL MANAGER **STAN KASTEN**
> EXPLAINING WHY HE WAS HAVING DIFFICULTY MAKING
> TRADES

"If we had one more center, we'd have one."

> SACRAMENTO KINGS COACH **JERRY REYNOLDS**, WHO WAS
> ANGRY AT MANAGEMENT'S DECISION TO TRADE CENTERS
> JOE KLEINE AND LASALLE THOMPSON WITHOUT GETTING A
> CENTER IN RETURN

"People like me."

> SEATTLE SUPERSONICS CENTER **DENNIS AWTREY** EXPLAINS
> WHY HE HAD BEEN TRADED SIX TIMES IN EIGHT YEARS

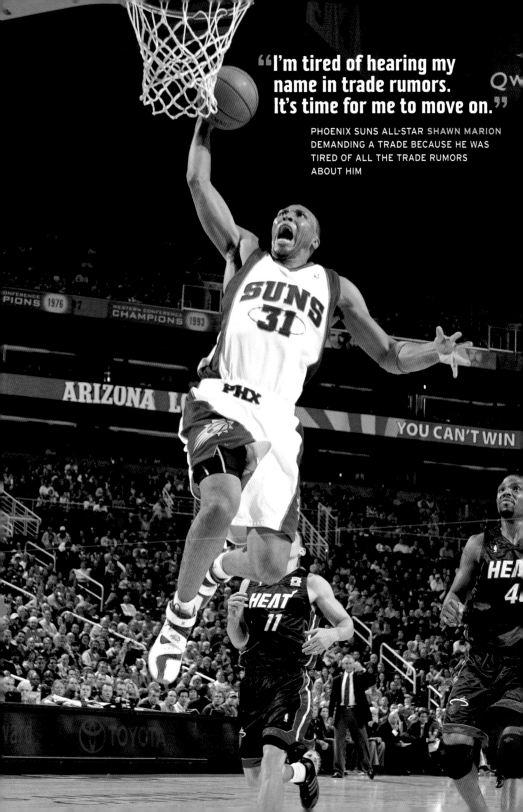

"I'm tired of hearing my name in trade rumors. It's time for me to move on."

PHOENIX SUNS ALL-STAR SHAWN MARION DEMANDING A TRADE BECAUSE HE WAS TIRED OF ALL THE TRADE RUMORS ABOUT HIM

"Ball handling and dribbling are my strongest weaknesses."

DENVER NUGGETS STAR **DAVID THOMPSON**

"Strength is my biggest weakness."

NEW MEXICO UNIVERSITY PLAYER **MARK SNOW**

"I don't like going to my right, but nobody knows that."

CONNECTICUT SUN FORWARD **KATIE DOUGLAS** OF THE WNBA

"The places where I need the most work are on my inside and outside games."

KANSAS CITY KING **DARNELL HILLMAN**

"The key is not the 'will to win' – everybody has that. It is the will to prepare to win that is important."

LEGENDARY NCAA COACH **BOBBY KNIGHT**

"Giving yourself permission to lose guarantees a loss."

MIAMI HEAT COACH **PAT RILEY**

"Winning is about having the whole team on the same page."

LEGENDARY PLAYER TURNED BROADCASTER **BILL WALTON**

"Everybody on a championship team doesn't get publicity, but everyone can say he's a champion."

LOS ANGELES LAKERS SUPERSTAR **MAGIC JOHNSON**

"When you're winning in a good environment everyone has your back. It's a world of difference."

EDDIE JONES, AFTER BEING TRADED FROM THE HOPELESSLY OUT OF IT MEMPHIS GRIZZLIES TO THE MIAMI HEAT IN 2007

"It's especially satisfying to know that we didn't just win, we dominated."

LOS ANGELES LAKER **RICK FOX** AFTER THE LAKERS STEAMROLLED THROUGH THE PLAYOFFS, GOING 15-1 TO CAPTURE THEIR SECOND STRAIGHT NBA CHAMPIONSHIP IN 2001

"Winning takes talent, to repeat takes character."

UCLA COACHING STAR **JOHN WOODEN**

"Talent wins games, but teamwork and intelligence wins championships."

CHICAGO BULLS SUPERSTAR **MICHAEL JORDAN**

"Those guys have established themselves. They've made their money, now what's left? They're not trying to make a name for themselves. Now the only thing for those guys is winning and how far you can get. With young players, they're trying to establish themselves. Making the All-Star team is important, making a certain amount of money is important, what everybody thinks of them is important. Those things don't weigh on your mind when you're a veteran player."

TORONTO RAPTORS COACH **SAM MITCHELL** ON WHY MOST CHAMPIONSHIP TEAMS NEED PLAYERS WITH AGE AND EXPERIENCE

"It never gets old. It only gets old if you lose."

BOSTON CELTICS GREAT **JOHN HAVLICEK** ON WINNING CHAMPIONSHIPS

"Personally, I just want to win a championship. There's nothing less than that. I don't care about just going to the playoffs; I've been to the playoffs before."

DENVER NUGGETS STAR **ALLEN IVERSON**

"The best team won. If you can't make it happen on the court, you don't deserve it."

LOS ANGELES LAKERS LEGEND **KAREEM ABDUL-JABBAR** AFTER THE LAKERS BEAT THE BOSTON CELTICS FOR THE 1984 NBA TITLE

"It was hard, but winning a championship is supposed to be hard. I think this is the way it was meant to be."

CHICAGO BULLS SUPERSTAR **MICHAEL JORDAN** AFTER BEATING THE SEATTLE SUPERSONICS IN THE 1996 NBA FINALS

"The zero is a powerful statement. It is for anybody who feels unappreciated or feels like someone is telling them that they are worth nothing."

GILBERT ARENAS, WHO WEARS NUMBER 0 FOR THE
WASHINGTON WIZARDS

"You go with the zero when you've been through something, and you are looking to get a new beginning. It helps you get going again. It helps you get the swag back."

UCLA GUARD RUSSELL WESTBROOK, WHO WORE NUMBER 0
AS A FRESHMAN IN 2006-07

"No matter who you are, wearing the number means something. It means that you've got to be more than a zero."

OREGON GUARD AARON BROOKS, WHO STARRED IN THE
NCAA WEARING NUMBER 0 IN 2006-07 AND CONTINUED
WEARING IT AS A ROOKIE WITH THE HOUSTON ROCKETS
IN 2007-08

cover: Victor Baldizon/NBAE via Getty Images; title page: Fernando Medina/NBAE via Getty Images; 8 Andrew D. Bernstein/1983 NBAE via Getty Images; 13 Focus on Sport/Getty Images; 15 Ken Regan/NBAE via Getty Images; 18 David Sandford/NBAE via Getty Images; 21 Joe Murphy/Getty Images; 24 Jerry Wachter/NBAE via Getty Images; 27 Neil Liefer/2004 NBAE via Getty Images; 28 Dick Raphael/1970 NBAE via Getty Images; 31 Stephen Dunn/Getty Images; 37 Rich Clarkson /Allsport/Getty Images; 38 Dick Raphael/1978 NBAE via Getty Images; 40 Andrew D. Bernstein/2005 NBAE via Getty Images; 45 Mike Fiala/AFP/Getty Images; 46 John Ruthroff/AFP/Getty Images; 49 Victor Baldizon/2006 NBAE via Getty Images; 50 Noah Graham/2007 NBAE via Getty Images; 57 Gregory Shamus/2005 NBAE via Getty Images; 58 Streeter Lecka/Getty Images; 61 Dick Raphael/1980 NBAE via Getty Images; 64 Jesse D. Garrabrant/2008 NBAE via Getty Images; 68 Wen Roberts/1970 NBAE via Getty Images; 71 Andrew D. Bernstein/ NBAE/ Getty Images; 76 Stan Honda/AFP/Getty Images; 83 Jesse D. Garrabrant/2007 NBAE via Getty Images; 87 Aaron Harris/AFP/ Getty Images; 92 Brian Bahr/Allsport/Getty Images; 95 Andrew D. Bernstein/2005 NBAE via Getty Images; 96 Andrew D. Bernstein/1986 NBAE via Getty Images; 101 Lou Capozzola/1990 NBAE/Getty Images; 102 James Nielsen/AFP/Getty Images; 107 Layne Murdoch/2007 NBAE via Getty Images; 110 Andrew D. Bernstein/2006 NBAE via Getty Images; 115 Andy Lyons/Getty Images; 118 Ronald Martinez/Getty Images; 123 Ken Levine/Allsport/Getty Images; 129 Jonathan Daniel/Allsport/Getty Images; 130 Lisa Blumenfeld/Getty Images; 134 David Liam Kyle/2008 NBAE via Getty Images; 137 Victor Baldizon/2007 NBAE via Getty Images; 139 Andrew D. Bernstein/2007 NBAE via Getty Images; 143 Nat Butler/2005 NBAE via Getty Images; 149 Jamie Squire/Getty Images; 152 Matt Campbell/AFP/Getty Images; 155 Nathaniel S. Butler/1998 NBAE via Getty Images; 158 Kent Smith/2008 NBAE via Getty Images; 163 Barry Gossage/2007 NBAE via Getty Images; 164 Jesse D. Garrabrant/2007 NBAE via Getty Images; 169 Garrett Ellwood/2008 NBAE/Getty Images; 170 Matthew Stockman/Getty Images

Eric Zweig is a managing editor with Dan Diamond and Associates, consulting publishers to the National Hockey League. A sports historian, he has written for many Canadian newspapers and is the author and editor of dozens of sports books, including four other "Quotes and Quips" titles. Though already 6 foot 1 as a young teenager, the realization that he was only as tall as Nate "Tiny" Archibald — and had no basketball talent — ended any dreams of an NBA career.